M000223677

Copyright (

Printed in the United States of America

First Printing, 2020

ISBN 978-1-7349568-3-2

Forest City Publications
1658 Milwaukee Ave # 100-16118
Chicago, IL 60647
www.forestcitypublications.com

POSITIVE

DISRUPTION

A QUOTE AND A QUESTION
TO UPSHIFT YOUR LIFE

TONY RUBLESKI

To the world.

Now is the time to get off our knees. Time to look at life with a renewed sense of possibility, not fear. Time for a new revolution, a positive disruption. Time to turn inward so we might rise upward. Time to solve the challenges now facing humanity by working on ourselves. Time to discover our inner genius, passion, and God-given talents.

INTRODUCTION

*"In the midst of chaos, there is
also opportunity."*
Sun Tzu

Someday…
Someday…
Someday…

That "someday" finally arrived on Mother's Day, May 10, 2020, at 1:11pm. That day I finally decided to unwrap a long-held dream in my heart by committing it into reality. It was time to take that dream from conception, create a 90-day deadline, and get working on it by starting the writing process. The main goal to craft it into physical form known as a book by 12/31/20 or sooner.

Little did I know that being forced off the road in mid-March due to covid-19 would essentially shut down my speaking business by early April, but that it would also force me to dig deep into my soul and turn everything over to God even more than I could imagine. The two questions that kept replaying over and over in my head were, God, where do I best use my talents? Where can I serve others who are scared, doubting their purpose, or looking at their life from a totally new perspective?

To adapt and deal with this new way of life and social distancing, which frankly I can't stand as a human who loves social connection, I employed long walks, journaling, reading, prayer, meditation, and staring at the bedroom ceiling many nights as the thoughts kept dropping in and out with sleep nowhere to be found. I was searching for a sign. A clue. An answer, or what I call a "God-wink" from the higher power.

The book you now hold is my response to how I feel I can help others dealing with this massive change on planet earth by creating something that has personally helped me during life's disruptions. As a writer, teacher, and avid reader, I've had the vision of writing a book containing my favorite quotes as a "do before you die" goal for many years. Confession time: My name is Tony. I'm a quote addict. Check out my social media pages over the past 10+ years and it quickly becomes apparent that I'm not joking!

There's something magical about a great quote at the right time. It almost seems like divine intervention when the words match a situation I'm facing or have experienced during my life journey. A great quote reminds us that we are not alone. That our shared humanity is real. That life has happened before us. That life is happening right now, and that life will still be going on long after we've exited the earthly plane.

The Goal of This Book

The number-one goal of this book is to help you get hooked on two core ideas you may have forgotten or never considered using daily to improve your life:

1. The simple power of a quote to shift your perception
2. The power of a question to change your mind and inspire action

I believe it's time to start consistently and daily taking better care of ourselves. To stop being the martyr. To save you from one of two groups that far too many people have no idea they joined or are members of:

#1: Over-Givers Anonymous
#2. Apathy Anonymous

Unfortunately, a lot of folks sadly come to realize many years later that they were a part of one group or the other. This shows up when they burn out physically, spiritually, or mentally from either giving away too much by being an excessive people-pleaser or, on the flip side, they selfishly give up and stop giving a damn about others or life in general. These two extremes are dangerous.

This book is simple by design.
The world is already complex enough.
This book is about your journey, your unique story.

It employs a daily quote and question to prompt you to turn inward for a few minutes each day. To cultivate your spirit and encourage you to dream again, to push yourself higher, and to use the power of questions to dig into your inner talents, genius, and passion to enrich your life and then unselfishly share it with others.

This book is about self-reflection. To move you into action by writing down what's buried deep in your heart and soul. To use it as a guide to help you improve your life even more and share it with

others. Let this book hook and anchor you into a new habit by self-reflecting daily and taking action to create your own Positive Disruption.

It's time for each of us to remove doubt, haters, and fear from our minds. To bring back the forgotten seven-year-old in each of us, who years earlier, thought and felt that anything was possible. To unhook from the play-it-safe mentality, the conforming majority of talking heads, and the negativity swirling around us on social media that made it acceptable and normal to downplay our passion, ideas, and life force in the name of comfort and security. To wake people up again to the fact that by suppressing our talents, ideas, and love for one another, we would be committing the biggest crime a human can face: A life of regret.

"As you rise above the sordid self; as you break, one after another, the chains that bind you, will you realize the joy of giving, as distinguished from the misery of grasping, giving of your substance; giving of your intellect; giving of the love and light that is growing within you. You will then understand that it is indeed "more blessed to give than to receive." But the giving must be of the heart without any taint of self, without the desire for reward.

The gift of pure love is always attended with bliss. If, after you have given, you are wounded because you are not thanked or flattered or your name put in the paper, know then that your gift was prompted by vanity and not by love, and you were merely giving in order to get, were not really giving but grasping.

Lose yourself in the welfare of others; forget yourself in all that you do; this is the secret of abounding happiness. Ever be on the watch to guard against selfishness, and learn faithfully the divine lessons of inward sacrifice; so shall you climb the highest heights of happiness and shall remain in the never-clouded sunshine of universal joy, clothed in the shining garment of immortality." -James Allen, 1901 (*From Poverty to Power*)

Under the Tree…I would be remiss if I didn't include this photo in the book.

It's a wonderful reminder to me that when disruption of the not so positive kind happens in our lives we are challenged when we least expect it. But, we always get to choose how we will deal with it, either proactively or negatively. In mid-June, a little over a month into writing this book, that exact scenario crashed into my life without warning. Sounds like 2020 for all of us, right?

I was forced to dig deep. To re-focus quickly and lock in on the original goal of getting this book manuscript done in 90 days. The real test was now looking at me face-to-face to see if I'd honor the goal, or capitulate and take a break. I knew if a quick decision wasn't made, that the goal of completing the book would likely be in jeopardy and frankly that it might die and never be finished. Would I focus on the painful setback or would I decide to move ahead with the mission? The answer came quickly and with a unique surprise.

The Tree, as I affectionately call it, became a key driver in this book being completed. The summer days were beautiful this year in West Michigan after a long, gray, and confining spring where the month of April alone seemed like it would never end. In late June I decided to take a walk in downtown Grand Haven, carrying a beach towel, notebook, pen, and my lunch. I parked myself in a nice shaded spot under my favorite tree and started writing. Little did I know that it would be exactly what I needed to get back on the horse and get moving. Within a few days something clicked and thereafter my daily appointment at the Tree to write and calm my mind was locked in.

The Tree became my safe space. A calm refuge to mediate, to eat, to listen to music, to think, to pray, and to write. It was also a welcome escape from a confused and scared world, the summer heat, and the pain that was pent up inside me. It was a healthy tranquilizer to quell the pain and deep disappointment. Under the Tree was where I made the daily decision to look ahead, not behind at what used to be. To move from dark to light.

As the quotes were selected for inclusion, and the questions were penned to go with them, my spirits picked up daily in tandem with the warm glow of summer. Time melted away. I'd often write for an hour to two hour each day and it seemed like five minutes. After each session, I found myself feeling inspired, alive, and renewed.

The unique combination of the writing, the cool breeze, the people walking by with happy faces, the sounds of the birds, the boats slowly passing by, and the stunning view of the pier and harbor became my daily place for creativity and healing. Yes, they contributed mightily to this book in ways that I could not have seen or imagined. Thank you, God, for the unforeseen surprise you dropped on me on a warm June day: the Tree.

Let's get started, shall we?

Tony Rubleski
October 2020

JANUARY

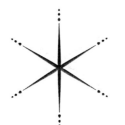

JANUARY 1

"THE NEW YEAR STANDS BEFORE
US, LIKE A CHAPTER IN A BOOK,
WAITING TO BE WRITTEN."
MELODY BEATTIE

What's a big goal, project, or dream
you need to take action on in the
upcoming new year?

_____

_____

_____

_____

_____

_____

JANUARY 2

"THE ONLY PERSON YOU ARE
DESTINED TO BECOME IS THE
PERSON YOU DECIDE TO BE."
RALPH WALDO EMERSON

What big decision have you been
delaying, that would excite if you
finally made it?

_____

_____

_____

_____

_____

_____

JANUARY 3

"YOU ARE NEVER TOO OLD TO
REINVENT YOURSELF."
STEVE HARVEY

What new class, skill, book, podcast,
online course, or hobby could you get
started on pursuing today?

_____

_____

_____

_____

_____

_____

JANUARY 4

"WE ALL HAVE TWO CHOICES:
WE CAN MAKE A LIVING OR WE
CAN DESIGN A LIFE."
JIM ROHN

Are you creating the life you truly
want, or stuck in a rut of what other
people want you to do or be?

_____

_____

_____

_____

_____

_____

JANUARY 5

"THE SIX BEST DOCTORS:
SUNSHINE, WATER, REST, AIR,
EXERCISE, AND DIET."
WAYNE FIELDS

Which of these doctors do you visit daily, and which one is overdue for a check-up?

_____

_____

_____

_____

_____

_____

JANUARY 6

"YOU ADAPT. YOU OVERCOME.
YOU IMPROVISE."
GUNNY HIGHWAY

For a major challenge you're currently facing, have you explored several options to solve it?

_____

_____

_____

_____

_____

_____

JANUARY 7

"GOD GAVE YOU THE GIFT OF
86,400 SECONDS TODAY. HAVE
YOU USED ONE TO SAY 'THANK
YOU'?"
WILLIAM WARD

Who are three people you can call,
text, or surprise with a thank you
message today?

JANUARY 8

"IF EVERYTHING AROUND YOU
SEEMS DARK. LOOK AGAIN, YOU
MAY BE THE LIGHT."
RUMI

Do you often turn inward through
prayer or meditation to seek calm and
serenity to improve your life?

JANUARY 9

"THERE IS NO REASON TO
CONSTANTLY ATTEMPT TO
FIGURE EVERYTHING OUT."
MICHAEL SINGER

Do you overthink or try to do too
much?

_____

_____

_____

_____

_____

_____

JANUARY 10

"RESISTANCE IS YOUR SIGNAL
THAT CHANGE IS HAPPENING."
JOHN ASSARAF

What person or life situation has been
consuming you lately, that needs to
be properly addressed and dealt with?

_____

_____

_____

_____

_____

_____

JANUARY 11

"DON'T WAIT FOR MIRACLES,
YOUR WHOLE LIFE IS A
MIRACLE."
ALBERT EINSTEIN

Are you focused on your blessings
more each day, or do you let worry
cloud your thinking and joy?

JANUARY 12

"YOU CAN'T WAIT FOR
INSPIRATION. YOU HAVE TO GO
AFTER IT WITH A CLUB."
JACK LONDON

What's one step you could take today
toward a major goal to get positive
momentum in motion?

_____

_____

_____

_____

_____

_____

"YOUR BEST DEFENSE IS A
STRONGER YOU."
C.J. ORTIZ

What one thing are you planning or
intend to do today to take better care
of your body, mind, and spirit?

_____

_____

_____

_____

_____

_____

JANUARY 14

"ARTISTS GIVE PEOPLE
SOMETHING THEY DIDN'T KNOW
THEY WERE MISSING."
DANIEL PINK

What movie, art, song or area of your
life gives you great joy that you
should experience today no matter
how busy your schedule?

JANUARY 15

"NEVER DOWNPLAY THE
SIGNIFICANCE OF YOUR OWN LIFE
STORY AND THE POSITIVE IMPACT
IT CAN HAVE ON OTHERS."
TONY RUBLESKI

What lesson(s) in your own life
shaped you positively that you can
share with others to inspire and
uplift?

JANUARY 16

"THE SECRET TO CHANGE IS TO
FOCUS ALL OF YOUR ENERGY NOT
ON FIGHTING THE OLD, BUT ON
BUILDING THE NEW."
SOCRATES

What key area in your life needs to be
examined to let go of and be replaced
with something new and better?

_____

_____

_____

_____

_____

_____

JANUARY 17

"LEAVING SOME THINGS UNDONE
IS A NECESSARY TRADE-OFF FOR
EXTRAORDINARY RESULTS."
GARY KELLER

Make a list of 10 things you need to stop doing in your life the next six-months. How would it feel if you started to remove these annoyances?

JANUARY 18

"IF YOU CAN'T FLY, THEN RUN, IF
YOU CAN'T RUN, THEN WALK, IF
YOU CAN'T WALK, THEN CRAWL,
BUT WHATEVER YOU DO, YOU
HAVE TO KEEP MOVING FORWARD."
MARTIN LUTHER KING, JR.

What proactive step can you take
today to improve your life in an area
that you enjoy?

JANUARY 19

"IF IT'S BEYOND YOUR POWER
TO CONTROL, LET IT GO."
EPICTETUS

What person or past experience do
you need to forgive and move on with
to achieve greater peace?

_____

_____

_____

_____

_____

_____

JANUARY 20

"KEEP SOME ROOM IN YOUR
HEART FOR THE UNIMAGINABLE."
MARY OLIVER

What dream, trip, adventure, project
or goal have you pushed off too long
that you should revisit pursuing?

_____

_____

_____

_____

_____

_____

JANUARY 21

"TIME. WASTING IT IS EASY UNTIL
YOU DO NOT HAVE ANY LEFT."
RICHARD B. BROOKE

If you knew today was your last day,
how would you spend it and who
would you reach out to say "I love
you" too?

JANUARY 22

"I JUST GOT TO A POINT WHERE I
DECIDED THAT I WANT TO LIVE
AN UNBULLSHITAFIED LIFE."
STEVE MARABOLI

What new boundary do you need to
exercise today with someone in your
life that is bringing you down or
causing excessive stress?

JANUARY 23

"YOU DON'T HAVE TO BE POSITIVE ALL THE TIME. IT'S PERFECTLY OKAY TO FEEL SAD, ANGRY, ANNOYED, FRUSTRATED, SCARED, OR ANXIOUS. HAVING FEELINGS DOESN'T MAKE YOU A 'NEGATIVE PERSON'. IT MAKES YOU HUMAN." LORI DESCHENE

What lessons are you learning from a tough day, person or event, to gain insight?

_____

_____

_____

_____

_____

_____

JANUARY 24

"THE GREATEST PRISON PEOPLE
LIVE IN, IS THE FEAR OF WHAT
OTHER PEOPLE THINK."
DAVID ICKE

Who are a couple of people in your
life that have too much say in your
life, that need to stop, or remove from
your mind or life?

_____

_____

_____

_____

_____

_____

JANUARY 25

"GET BUSY LIVING, OR GET BUSY
DYING."
STEPHEN KING

Does the day ahead of you feel like it
will be boring, unpleasant, average,
or exciting with what it may hold?

JANUARY 26

"LEARN TO STAY INSIDE THE
GRACE OF JUST ONE DAY.
EVERYTHING ELSE IS AN
IMAGINATION."
WILLIAM PAUL YOUNG

Do you look back too much or jump
ahead with your thoughts on a typical
day?

JANUARY 27

"THE MEDIOCRE TEACHER TELLS.
THE GOOD TEACHER EXPLAINS.
THE SUPERIOR TEACHER
DEMONSTRATES. THE GREAT
TEACHER INSPIRES."
WILLIAM ARTHUR WARD

Who are two or three great mentors,
teachers, or coaches in your life that
have positively influenced your life
journey and why?

_____

_____

_____

_____

_____

_____

JANUARY 28

"GRATITUDE IS NOT ONLY THE
GREATEST OF VIRTUES, BUT THE
PARENT OF ALL OTHERS."
CICERO

No matter how you're feeling as you
read this. List five major things you
are grateful for at this time within
your life?

_____

_____

_____

_____

_____

_____

JANUARY 29

"I'VE NEVER MET A STRONG
PERSON WITH AN EASY PAST."
ATTICUS

Are you too comfortable with life or
are you pushing to grow and get
outside your comfort zone?

_____

_____

_____

_____

_____

_____

JANUARY 30

"TREASURE THIS DAY AND TREASURE YOURSELF. TRULY, NEITHER WILL EVER HAPPEN AGAIN." -RAY BRADBURY

Will you get and give from today or regret and take it for granted?

JANUARY 31

"IF YOU SPEND TOO MUCH TIME
THINKING ABOUT A THING,
YOU'LL NEVER GET IT DONE."
BRUCE LEE

What's the biggest goal or dream
you've put off too long, that you need
to make a priority now?

_____

_____

_____

_____

_____

_____

FEBRUARY

FEBRUARY 1

"LOVE DIFFICULT PEOPLE.
YOU ARE ONE OF THEM."
BOB GOFF

Are you quick to judge or get
impatient with others? If yes, what
can you do right now to be more
patient and extend more empathy?

_____

_____

_____

_____

_____

FEBRUARY 2

"HOW YOU DEAL WITH FAILURE
DETERMINES WHETHER OR NOT
YOU EVER GET THE OPPORTUNITY
TO DEAL WITH SUCCESS."
DAN S. KENNEDY

What abandoned goal or project do
you need to dust off, revisit, and look
into completing by taking action
towards today?

_____

_____

_____

_____

_____

_____

FEBRUARY 3

"YOU JUST CAN'T BEAT THE
PERSON WHO NEVER GIVES UP."
BABE RUTH

Do you quit or get frustrated easily
when facing a major challenge, or do
you look for new ideas and options to
solve it?

FEBRUARY 4

"HOW PEOPLE TREAT YOU IS
THEIR KARMA. HOW YOU REACT
IS YOURS."
WAYNE DYER

Do you take things too personally, or
are you flexible with how you interact
with others?

_____

_____

_____

_____

_____

_____

FEBRUARY 5

"IT'S ABOUT PROGRESS, NOT
BEING PERFECT."
JEFF WALKER

Do you take immediate action when
you make a decision, or do you tend
to overthink?

_____

_____

_____

_____

_____

_____

FEBRUARY 6

"THE ELIMINATION DIET: REMOVE
ANGER, REGRET, WORRY,
RESENTMENT, GUILT AND BLAME.
THEN WATCH YOUR HEALTH AND
LIFE IMPROVE."
CHARLES GLASSMAN

Which one of these listed, do you
need to circle and on eliminating
starting today?

_____

_____

_____

_____

_____

_____

FEBRUARY 7

"BEGIN EACH DAY WITH
GRATITUDE AND MORE BLESSINGS
WILL FLOW INTO YOUR LIFE."
DAMIEN THOMAS

How do you start and end most days?

_____

_____

_____

_____

_____

_____

FEBRUARY 8

"IN THREE WORDS I CAN SUM UP
EVERYTHING I'VE LEARNED
ABOUT LIFE: IT GOES ON."
ROBERT FROST

What major setback in your life did
you grow from that at the time,
seemed like it would never be solved?

_____

_____

_____

_____

_____

_____

FEBRUARY 9

"GIVE THANKS FOR BLESSINGS EVERY
DAY. EVERYDAY. EMBRACE GRATITUDE.
ENCOURAGE OTHERS. IT IS IMPOSSIBLE
TO BE GRATEFUL AND HATEFUL AT
THE SAME TIME."
DENZEL WASHINGTON

Stop and think of five people within
your life that bring you joy, love, and
laughter.

_____

_____

_____

_____

_____

_____

FEBRUARY 10

"DEFINITENESS OF PURPOSE IS THE
STARTING POINT OF ALL
ACHIEVEMENT."
W. CLEMENT STONE

Do you consider yourself happy or
questioning your life path and career?

_____

_____

_____

_____

_____

_____

FEBRUARY 11

"REPETITION MAKES THE MASTER."
MUHAMMED ALI

What habit, if added into your life, could have a positive effect on multiple levels?

_____

_____

_____

_____

_____

_____

FEBRUARY 12

"EVERYTHING YOU WANT IS ON
THE OTHER SIDE OF FEAR."
JACK CANFIELD

What big fear is weighing on your
mind that you could move towards
solving starting now?

_____

_____

_____

_____

_____

_____

FEBRUARY 13

"GIVE YOURSELF PERMISSION TO
CUT NEGATIVE PEOPLE FROM YOUR
LIFE AND SURROUND YOURSELF
WITH PEOPLE WHO BRING OUT THE
BEST IN YOU."
JAMES ALTUCHER

Who in your life takes far too much
of your time and energy to the
detriment of helping others?

_____

_____

_____

_____

_____

_____

FEBRUARY 14

"LIVE EVERY DAY LIKE IT'S YOUR
SECOND CHANCE AT LIFE."
VIKTOR FRANKL

Will you take today for granted or as
a blessing?

_____

_____

_____

_____

_____

_____

FEBRUARY 15

"MOST PEOPLE SEEK A 60-SECOND
ANSWER TO A 10-YEAR PROBLEM."
TONY RUBLESKI

Do you consider yourself a patient or
impatient person?

_____

_____

_____

_____

_____

_____

FEBRUARY 16

"WE ARE REMINDED HOW SHORT
LIFE REALLY IS, AND HOW WE ARE
JUST PASSING THROUGH. SO, ALL
THE PEOPLE YOU HAVEN'T TOLD
YOU LOVE LATELY, TELL THEM, AND
LIVE YOUR DAYS LIKE YOU MEAN IT."
HAL SUTTON

Who is someone you need to reach out
to today to tell them how much you
love and respect them?

_____

_____

_____

_____

_____

_____

FEBRUARY 17

"DON'T LET SOMEONE ELSE'S
OPINION OF YOU BECOME YOUR
REALITY."
LES BROWN

Do you take criticism too seriously,
or do you live most of your days
without worry of others opinions?

_____

_____

_____

_____

_____

_____

FEBRUARY 18

"TO ACCOMPLISH GREAT THINGS
WE MUST NOT ONLY ACT, BUT
ALSO DREAM; NOT ONLY PLAN,
BUT ALSO BELIEVE."
ANATOLE FRANCE

What major goal are you taking action
on now that will dramatically improve
your life?

FEBRUARY 19

"THE MIND ONCE STRETCHED BY
A NEW IDEA, NEVER RETURNS TO
ITS ORIGINAL DIMENSIONS."
RALPH WALDO EMERSON

What new information or skill have
you learned in the past few days that
has improved your life?

_____

_____

_____

_____

_____

_____

FEBRUARY 20

"GRATITUDE IN ADVANCE IS THE
MOST POWERFUL CREATIVE
FORCE IN THE UNIVERSE."
NEALE DONALD WALSH

Do you give thanks for what you
currently have going well in your life,
or do you often focus on what's
missing?

_____

_____

_____

_____

_____

FEBRUARY 21

"WORKING HARD FOR SOMETHING
WE DON'T CARE ABOUT IS
CALLED STRESS. WORKING HARD
FOR SOMETHING WE LOVE IS
CALLED PASSION."
SIMON SINEK

Is your present job or vocation creating undue stress or does it give you a sense of satisfaction even on tough days?

_____

_____

_____

_____

_____

_____

FEBRUARY 22

"CONTINUOUS LEARNING IS THE
MINIMUM REQUIREMENT FOR
SUCCESS IN YOUR FIELD. LEARN
SOMETHING NEW EVERY DAY."
BRIAN TRACY

What will you do today to upgrade
your knowledge and get better in your
profession?

_____

_____

_____

_____

_____

_____

FEBRUARY 23

"PERSEVERANCE IS NOT A LONG
RACE; IT IS MANY SHORT RACES
ONE AFTER ANOTHER."
WALTER ELLIOTT

Do you break down tasks well or do
you spend time worrying about the
process and where to even start?

_____

_____

_____

_____

_____

_____

FEBRUARY 24

"LIFE IS NOT A DRESS
REHEARSEL. EVERYDAY, YOU
SHOULD HAVE AT LEAST ONE
EXQUISITE MOMENT."
SALLY KARLOTH

Are you just getting by each day, or
are you looking at it with a positive
and open-minded approach?

FEBRUARY 25

"FAITH IS TAKING THE FIRST STEP
EVEN WHEN YOU DON'T SEE THE
WHOLE STAIRCASE."
MARTIN LUTHER KING, JR.

What risk or leap of faith do you need
to take today within your life instead
of delaying?

_____

_____

_____

_____

_____

_____

FEBRUARY 26

"SOMEWHERE, SOMEONE IS
LOOKING FOR EXACTLY WHAT
YOU HAVE TO OFFER."
LOUISE HAY

Do you give up too soon, or do you
persist on looking for new options
and ideas to help you serve more
people?

_____

_____

_____

_____

_____

_____

FEBRUARY 27

"ORDINARY RICHES CAN BE STOLEN,
REAL RICHES CANNOT. IF YOUR SOUL
ARE INFINITELY PRECIOUS THINGS
THAT CANNOT BE TAKEN FROM
YOU."
OSCAR WILDE

What are five things in your life that
give you great joy and satisfaction
when you think about them?

_____

_____

_____

_____

_____

_____

FEBRUARY 28

"ALL ANY TEACHER CAN DO IS
TO AWAKEN THAT WHICH IS
ALREADY WITHIN YOU."
JOSEPH MURPHY

What skill, hobby, or area of interest
in your life do you need to find a
teacher or coach to help you grow?

MARCH

MARCH 1

"I WILL NEVER QUIT. I PERSEVERE
AND THRIVE ON ADVERSITY. IF
KNOCKED DOWN, I WILL GET
BACK UP, EVERY TIME."
U.S NAVY SEALS

What challenge or task will you bravely face today and get done no matter what?

_____

_____

_____

_____

_____

_____

MARCH 2

"SET YOUR MIND ON A DEFINITE
GOAL AND OBSERVE HOW
QUICKLY THE WORLD STANDS
ASIDE TO LET YOU PASS."
NAPOLEON HILL

What big goal have you been working
on that is moving ahead better than
you originally thought?

_____

_____

_____

_____

_____

_____

MARCH 3

"NEGATIVITY KILLS YOU. NEVER
FORGET THAT. IT'S A WEED THAT
EVENTUALLY CHOKES YOU TO
DEATH."
STUART WILDE

What negative person in your life who
drains your energy and focus, do you
need to spend less time with or taking
a break?

_____

_____

_____

_____

_____

_____

MARCH 4

"WHEN A PERSON IS DOWN IN THE WORLD, AN OUNCE OF HELP IS BETTER THAN A POUND OF PREACHING."
EDWARD LYTTON

How can you listen better today to meet people where they are at, instead of trying to fix them?

_____

_____

_____

_____

_____

_____

MARCH 5

"YOUR ATTITUDE, NOT YOUR
APTITUDE, WILL DETERMINE YOUR
ALTITUDE."
ZIG ZIGLAR

Do you consider yourself and the key
people in your life to be positive or
more pessimistic?

_____

_____

_____

_____

_____

_____

MARCH 6

"IT'S AMAZING WHAT YOU CAN
DO WHEN YOU'RE SUFFICIENTLY
INSPIRED."
BEN GAY III

What personal reasons do you use to
stay on task in pursuit of your major
goals?

_____

_____

_____

_____

_____

_____

MARCH 7

"OUR LIFE IS FRITTERED AWAY BY
DETAIL. SIMPLIFY, SIMPLIFY."
H. DAVID THOREAU

What is one time wasting thing you
do regularly that if you cut back or
eliminated completely, would bring
you greater peace of mind?

MARCH 8

"CONTINUOUS EFFORT, NOT
STRENGTH OR INTELLIGENCE, IS
THE KEY TO UNLOCKING OUR
POTENTIAL."
WINSTON CHURCHILL

What daily habit(s) do you employ to
get things done consistently?

_____

_____

_____

_____

_____

_____

MARCH 9

"I HAVE SPENT MOST OF MY LIFE
UNLEARNING THINGS THAT WERE
PROVED NOT TO BE TRUE."
BUCKMINSTER FULLER

When was the last time you
challenged a belief in your life that
doesn't make sense?

_____

_____

_____

_____

_____

_____

MARCH 10

"CONFLICT CANNOT SURVIVE
WITHOUT YOUR PARTICIPATION."
WAYNE DYER

Are you drawn to gossip and drama
from the same people or do you watch
who you associate and listen to
carefully?

MARCH 11

"BEAUTY IS HOW YOU FEEL
INSIDE, AND IT REFLECTS IN
YOUR EYES. IT IS NOT
SOMETHING PHYSICAL."
SOPHIA LOREN

What can you do today that inspires
you and brings you greater joy?

_____

_____

_____

_____

_____

_____

MARCH 12

"WE MAY THINK THAT WE FULLY CONTROL OURSELVES. HOWEVER, A FRIEND CAN EASILY REVEAL SOMETHING ABOUT US THAT WE HAVE ABSOLUTELY NO IDEA ABOUT." CARL JUNG

Do you surround yourself with honest friends who aren't afraid to support you, but also call you out when needed?

MARCH 13

"A DAY WITHOUT LAUGHTER IS A
DAY WASTED."
CHARLIE CHAPLIN

Children laugh hundreds of times a
day. Do you seek out laughter daily or
are you too serious and uptight?

_____

_____

_____

_____

_____

_____

MARCH 14

"IN THE END IT'S NOT THE YEARS
IN YOUR LIFE THAT COUNT, IT'S
THE LIFE IN THOSE YEARS."
ABRAHAM LINCOLN

What old hobby or passion do you
need to look at adding back into your
life?

_____

_____

_____

_____

_____

_____

MARCH 15

"THE CRITIC REVELS AND ENJOYS
SPENDING TIME PICKING APART
YOUR DREAM VERSUS WORKING
ON THEIR OWN."
TONY RUBLESKI

What will you do today, even in the
face of criticism, to keep moving
forward in your life?

_____

_____

_____

_____

_____

_____

MARCH 16

"LEARNING TO LISTEN IS THE
ESSENCE OF INTELLIGENT
LIVING."
SADHGURU

If the big gifts you give others are
your attention and time, do you honor
others by truly listening more than
talking?

MARCH 17

"YOU WILL BECOME AS SMALL OR
AS YOUR CONTROLLING DESIRE;
AS GREAT AS YOUR DOMINANT
ASPIRATION."
JAMES ALLEN

What are you really good at that if
you spent an extra 15-20 minutes a
day on, would propel you to even
greater satisfaction and joy?

MARCH 18

"A MAN OF COURAGE IS ALSO
FULL OF FAITH."
CICERO

Do you count mainly on yourself, or
do you also employ others and the
Higher Power to carry you forward?

_____

_____

_____

_____

_____

_____

MARCH 19

In the sped up digital world, when's the last time you unplugged, got outside, and focused just on the present moment?

_____

_____

_____

_____

_____

MARCH 20

"GREAT MINDS DISCUSS IDEAS,
AVERAGE MINDS DISCUSS EVENTS;
SMALL MINDS DISCUSS PEOPLE."
ELEANOR ROOSEVELT

Are you focused on goals and projects
that truly inspire, or are you easily
distracted by people and things you
can't or shouldn't try to control?

MARCH 21

"TO HAVE FAITH IS TO TRUST
YOURSELF TO THE WATER. WHEN
YOU SWIM YOU DON'T GRAB HOLD
OF THE WATER, BECAUSE IF YOU DO
YOU WILL SINK AND DROWN.
INSTEAD YOU RELAX AND FLOAT."
ALAN WATTS

What can you do today to turn your
mind off and simply relax?

MARCH 22

"THE WEAK CAN NEVER FORGIVE.
FORGIVENESS IS THE ATTRIBUTE
OF THE STRONG."
GHANDI

Who do you need to finally forgive
and release from your life?

_____

_____

_____

_____

_____

_____

MARCH 23

"TO BE YOURSELF IN A WORLD THAT
IS CONSTANTLY TRYING TO MAKE
YOU SOMETHING ELSE IS THE
GREATEST ACCOMPLISHMENT."
EMERSON

Who are the positive people in your
life that consistently support and
encourage you?

_____

_____

_____

_____

_____

_____

MARCH 24

"NOTHING CAN ADD MORE POWER
TO YOUR LIFE THAN
CONCENTRATING ALL YOUR
ENERGIES ON A LIMITED SET OF
TARGETS."
NIDO QUBEIN

What are three key things that if you completed them today would be a relief and lower your stress?

MARCH 25

"THE GREATEST WEAPON
AGAINST STRESS IS OUR ABILITY
TO CHOOSE ONE THOUGHT OVER
ANOTHER."
WILLIAM JAMES

How do you keep yourself focused
when life seems to be crashing in at
certain times?

_____

_____

_____

_____

_____

_____

MARCH 26

"YOU CAN'T BE BRAVE IF YOU'VE
ONLY HAD WONDERFUL THINGS
HAPPEN TO YOU."
MARY TYLER MOORE

What wounds have you turned into
wisdom in your life?

_____

_____

_____

_____

_____

_____

MARCH 27

"PROCRASTINATION IS ONE OF THE
MOST COMMON AND DEADLIEST
DISEASES AND ITS TOLL ON SUCCESS
AND HAPPINESS IS HEAVY."
WAYNE GRETZKY

What key regret is weighing on you
that you want to solve starting today?

_____

_____

_____

_____

_____

_____

MARCH 28

"BEGIN DOING WHAT YOU WANT TO
DO NOW. WE ARE NOT LIVING IN
ETERNITY. WE HAVE ONLY THIS
MOMENT, SPARKLING LIKE A STAR IN
OUR HAND AND MELTING LIKE A
SNOWFLAKE."
FRANCIS BACON JR.

If you knew you might die in 24-
hours, what would you do differently
right now?

_____

_____

_____

_____

_____

_____

MARCH 29

"I FOUND EVERY SINGLE SUCCESSFUL
PERSON I'VE EVER SPOKEN TO HAD A
TURNING POINT AND THE TURNING
POINT WAS WHERE THEY MADE A
CLEAR, SPECIFIC, UNEQUIVOCAL
DECISION THAT THEY WERE NOT
GOING TO LIVE LIKE THIS ANYMORE."
BRIAN TRACY

What major moment of decision in
your life turned out to be of enormous
value?

_____

_____

_____

_____

_____

MARCH 30

"LET GO OR BE DRAGGED."
ZEN PROVERB

What unresolved piece within your
personal life do you need to finally
address and let go of starting today?

_____

_____

_____

_____

_____

_____

MARCH 31

"THERE ARE MORE THINGS TO
ALARM US THEN TO HARM US,
AND WE SUFFER MORE OFTEN IN
APPREHENSION THAN REALITY."
SENECA

How do you manage fear, gossip, and
doubt each day to keep pushing
forward?

APRIL

APRIL 1

"IF YOU ARE GOING TO DO
ANYTHING, YOU MUST EXPECT
CRITICISM. BUT IT'S BETTER TO BE A
DOER THAN A CRITIC. THE DOER
MOVES; THE CRITIC STANDS STILL
AND IS PASSED BY."
BRUCE BARTON

If we all have doubters, do you give
them too much focus, or do you turn
inward and still press onward?

_____

_____

_____

_____

_____

APRIL 2

"YOUR RESENTMENT OF ANOTHER
PERSON'S SUCCESS CURTAILS
YOUR OWN CHANCE OF
SUCCESS."
ECKHART TOLLE

Who in your world is happy and doing
well that you need to applaud more,
instead of being resentful towards?

APRIL 3

"THE AVERAGE PERSON IS ENTIRELY
INNOCENT OF ANY DEEP THINKING.
THEY ACCEPT THE IDEAS OF OTHERS
AND REPEAT THEM, IN VERY MUCH THE
SAME WAY AS A PARROT. CREATIVE
THINKING REQUIRES ATTENTION."
CHARLES HAANEL

What new knowledge have you picked
up recently that has challenged and
made you think?

APRIL 4

"IT IS ONLY WITH GRATITUDE
THAT LIFE BECOMES RICH."
DIETRICH BONHOEFFER

Is your daily mindset tilt more
towards gratitude or a sense of
entitlement?

APRIL 5

"NOT BEING EXCITED IS TO HAVE MISSED THE WHOLE POINT OF LIFE."
STEVE CHANDLER

When was the last time you really got fired up, excited, and truly inspired?

APRIL 6

"DON'T COMPARE YOURSELF
WITH OTHER PEOPLE; COMPARE
YOURSELF WITH WHO YOU WERE
YESTERDAY."
JORDAN PETERSON

Are you pushing yourself forward
each day to impress yourself, not
others? How can you do better?

APRIL 7

"STRENGTH DOES NOT COME FROM
WINNING. YOUR STRUGGLES DEVELOP
YOUR STRENGTHS. WHEN YOU GO
THROUGH HARDSHIPS AND DECIDE
NOT TO SURRENDER, THAT IS
STRENGTH."
ARNOLD SCHWARZENEGGER

What challenge or fear have you
overcome recently that has made you
stronger or better?

_____

_____

_____

_____

_____

_____

APRIL 8

"NEVER BE ASHAMED. THERE'S
SOME WHO'LL HOLD IT AGAINST
YOU, BUT THEY'RE NOT WORTH
BOTHERING WITH."
J.K. ROWLING

When has someone made you feel ashamed, though later, you realized it wasn't worth worrying about?

APRIL 9

"THE WORLD IS CHANGED BY
YOUR EXAMPLE, NOT BY YOUR
OPINION."
PAULO COELHO

Where is an area that you can lead by
example vs. by your words?

_____

_____

_____

_____

_____

_____

APRIL 10

"WHEN A CHILD IS LEARNING
HOW TO WALK AND FALLS DOWN
50 TIMES THEY NEVER THINK TO
THEMSELVES 'MAYBE THIS ISN'T
FOR ME."
RAY AHN

Describe a time that you failed repeatedly in your life but refused to be beaten and give up.

_____

_____

_____

_____

_____

_____

APRIL 11

"INNER PEACE BEGINS THE
MOMENT YOU CHOOSE NOT TO
ALLOW ANOTHER PERSON OR
EVENT TO CONTROL YOUR
EMOTIONS."
PEMA CHODRON

What do you do daily to achieve
greater inner peace?

APRIL 12

"SOME PEOPLE WILL NEVER LIKE
YOU BECAUSE YOUR SPIRIT
IRRITATES THEIR DEMONS."
DENZEL WASHINGTON

How do you know when it's time to
let someone go in order to preserve
your spirit?

_____

_____

_____

_____

_____

_____

APRIL 13

"IT IS A GREAT THING TO KNOW
THE SEASON FOR SPEECH AND
THE SEASON FOR SILENCE."
SENECA

Do you think before you respond, or
do you allow your emotions to
compulsively take over and speak
before it's your turn?

_____

_____

_____

_____

_____

APRIL 14

"CHARACTER IS THE ABILITY TO CARRY OUT A GOOD RESOLUTION LONG AFTER THE EXCITEMENT OF THE MOMENT HAS PASSED."
CAVETT ROBERT

Do you follow through on your commitments consistently or do you come up with excuses?

APRIL 15

"WHEN WE PUSH OUT DOUBT,
OUR INNER GENIUS HAS A
CHANCE TO SHINE."
TONY RUBLESKI

Do you watch what you think about
carefully and if it's either uplifting
your spirit or bringing you down?

APRIL 16

"BE IMPECCABLE WITH YOUR WORD.
SPEAK WITH INTEGRITY. SAY ONLY
WHAT YOU MEAN. AVOID USING THE
WORD TO SPEAK AGAINST YOURSELF
OR TO GOSSIP ABOUT OTHERS."
DON MIGUEL RUIZ

Do you find your internal dialogue to
be mostly positive or is it criticizing
and often too harsh?

APRIL 17

"THE MIND IS A VERY POWERFUL
TOOL THAT CAN WORK FOR OR
AGAINST YOU."
DAVE LINIGER

Do you monitor what goes into your
mind daily, from what you see, hear,
and feel, online and offline to the
main thoughts you think about daily?

_____

_____

_____

_____

_____

_____

APRIL 18

"INSTEAD OF WONDERING WHEN YOUR NEXT VACATION IS, MAYBE YOU SHOULD SET UP A LIFE YOU DON'T NEED TO ESCAPE FROM."
SETH GODIN

Do you enjoy what you do for a living, or do you feel stuck in rut and need to take a serious look at making a change?

APRIL 19

"LAZINESS MAY APPEAR
ATTRACTIVE, BUT WORK GIVES
SATISFACTION."
ANNE FRANK

Do you find yourself becoming lazy
several times a day instead of being
inspired?

_____

_____

_____

_____

_____

_____

APRIL 20

"THE MORE REAL YOU GET, THE
MORE UNREAL THE WORLD GETS."
JOHN LENNON

What old belief or story about your
life have you shed or let go of to
improve?

_____

_____

_____

_____

_____

_____

APRIL 21

"STRENGTH GROWS IN THE MOMENTS WHEN YOU CAN'T GO ON BUT YOU KEEP GOING ANYWAY."
ED MYLETT

What long-term goal have you achieved that seemed almost impossible at first, but once completed, was a major turning point?

APRIL 22

"GIVERS GAIN."
IVAN MISNER

When's the last time you did
something unexpected for another
person with no expectation of
anything in return?

APRIL 23

"SETTING GOALS IS THE FIRST
STEP IN TURNING THE INVISIBLE
INTO THE VISIBLE."
TONY ROBBINS

Are you drifting through life
comfortably or lazily, or are you
defining goals to push you toward a
more fulfilling life?

APRIL 24

"THE CONSTANT NEED TO MAKE
EVERYONE ELSE HAPPY AT THE
COST OF YOUR OWN HAPPINESS
WILL DESTROY YOU."
LARRY WINGET

Do you have boundaries that protect
and serve your peace-of-mind or do
you run yourself ragged trying to
make others happy?

APRIL 25

"ONLY THOSE WHO WILL RISK
GOING TOO FAR CAN POSSIBLY
FIND OUT HOW FAR THEY CAN
GO."
T.S. ELIOT

What major goal is pushing you to
risk growing outside of your current
comfort zone?

APRIL 26

"A RELATIONSHIP IS REBORN WHEN
WHENEVER WE SEE SOMEONE AS THEY
ARE RIGHT NOW AND DON'T HOLD THEM
TO WHO THEY WERE FOCUSING ON THE
PRESENT, NOT THE PAST, IS ESSENTIAL
TO THE EXPERIENCE OF GRACE."
MARIANNE WILLIAMSON

Who in your life do you need to
extend grace and acceptance toward
today?

APRIL 27

"PEOPLE WANT PROGRESS, BUT
THEY DON'T WANT CHANGE."
EVA BURROWS
AUSTRALIAN SALVATION ARMY
OFFICER

Are you open-minded to new ideas
and change, or do you consider
yourself fearful of change to the point
where you're stuck in outdated
habits?

_____

_____

_____

_____

_____

APRIL 28

"DECIDE WHAT YOU WANT.
BELIEVE YOU CAN HAVE IT.
BELIEVE YOU DESERVE IT.
BELIEVE IT'S POSSIBLE FOR
YOU."
RHONDA BYRNE

What major goal or dream would you pursue if you knew you could not fail?

APRIL 29

"THE MOST COMMON ONE-LINER
IN THE BIBLE IS, "DO NOT BE
AFRAID." SOMEONE COUNTED,
AND IT OCCURS 365 TIMES."
RICHARD ROHR

What daily fear do you need to
address and work toward letting go of
starting today?

_____

_____

_____

_____

_____

_____

APRIL 30

"THE FORGIVING STATE OF MIND
IS A MAGNETIC POWER FOR
ATTRACTING GOOD."
CATHERINE PONDER

Who or what do you need to forgive
to uplift your spirit?

MAY

MAY 1

"IT IS BETTER TO BE IN THE ARENA, GETTING STOMPED BY THE BULL, THEN TO BE UP IN THE STANDS OR OUT IN THE PARKING LOT."
STEVEN PRESSFIELD

How do you deal with critics online and in-person so you can move "into the arena?"

MAY 2

"YOU ARE NEVER TOO OLD TO
SET ANOTHER GOAL OR DREAM A
NEW DREAM."
C.S. LEWIS

What goals and dreams do you have
for yourself that you are currently
pursuing?

_____

_____

_____

_____

_____

_____

MAY 3

"TO BE LOVED MEANS TO BE
RECOGNIZED AS EXISTING."
THICH NHAT HANH

Who needs a long overdue call, text,
or in-person visit from you to say
"hello" and check up on them?

_____

_____

_____

_____

_____

_____

MAY 4

"THE GREATEST DAY IN YOUR
LIFE AND MINE IS WHEN WE TAKE
TOTAL RESPONSIBILITY FOR OUR
ATTITUDES. THAT'S THE DAY WE
TRULY GROW UP."
JOHN MAXWELL

What pity party or resentment do you
need to acknowledge and let go of
which you know is holding you back?

_____

_____

_____

_____

_____

_____

MAY 5

"AS CHILDREN, WE WERE AFRAID
OF THE DARK. NOW AS ADULTS,
WE ARE AFRAID OF THE LIGHT.
WE ARE AFRAID TO STEP OUT.
WE ARE AFRAID TO BECOME
MORE." ANDY ANDREWS

When's the last time you took a leap
of faith and ignored the fear of doubt
in your mind?

MAY 6

"THERE ARE NO VICTIMS, ONLY
VOLUNTEERS."
LEE MILTEER

What negative story in your mind do
you need to work on removing today?

_____

_____

_____

_____

_____

_____

MAY 7

"THOUGHT IS ENERGY. MENTAL IMAGES ARE CONCENTRATED ENERGY. AND ENERGY CONCENTRATED ON ANY DEFINITE PURPOSE BECOMES POWER." ROBERT COLLIER

Are you focused more each day on what's going well in your life and where you're heading, versus looking into the past?

MAY 8

"IF YOU'RE BUILDING A HOUSE OR
DOING ANYTHING, TIME IS WHAT
YOU'VE GOT. WELL. THERE'S EFFORT,
BUT YOU NEED TIME. THE MORE TIME
YOU PUT INTO SOMETHING, THE
BETTER STUFF YOU CAN MAKE."
GENE SIMMONS

Are you patient in pursuit of your
goals or do you try to rush every step
without giving each one better focus
and effort?

MAY 9

"EVERYONE WANTS TO BE
APPRECIATED, SO IF YOU
APPRECIATE SOMEONE, DON'T
KEEP IT A SECRET."
MARY KAY ASH

Who do you appreciate and how can
you let them know today?

_____

_____

_____

_____

_____

MAY 10

"CHANGE IS INEVITABLE BUT
PERSONAL GROWTH IS A
CHOICE."
BOB PROCTOR

Do you approach each day with a
sense of adventure and learning or
with apprehension?

_____

_____

_____

_____

_____

_____

MAY 11

"SOME PEOPLE CHASE
HAPPINESS. AND SOME PEOPLE
CHOOSE HAPPINESS."
ROBERT HOLDEN

Will you approach this day chasing or choosing happiness?

MAY 12

"RAISE YOUR WORDS, NOT YOUR
VOICE. IT IS RAIN THAT GROWS
FLOWERS, NOT THUNDER."
RUMI

Do you consider yourself to be
impatient or calm when interacting
with others?

_____

_____

_____

_____

_____

_____

MAY 13

"CREATIVITY IS GOD'S GIFT TO
US. USING OUR CREATIVITY IS
OUR GIFT BACK TO GOD."
JULIA CAMERON

Are you growing and expanding your
talents to better serve others, or are
you stuck in a rut of familiarity?

_____

_____

_____

_____

_____

_____

MAY 14

"PEACE, BE STILL."
JESUS

When's the last time you took 15 solid minutes to unwind, not rush and center the thoughts within your mind?

MAY 15

"GUARD YOUR MIND EACH DAY
FROM NEGATIVE PEOPLE, NEWS,
AND GOSSIP."
TONY RUBLESKI

How much time do you spend on
average each day with social media,
news, and interacting with friends
who take more than they give? How
can you lessen this?

_____

_____

_____

_____

_____

MAY 16

"LAUGHTER IS A MOMENTARY
HOLIDAY."
JUDY JOHNSON

Are you taking a few "laughter
holidays" every day?

_____

_____

_____

_____

_____

_____

MAY 17

"THE MOST WASTED OF ALL DAYS
IS WITHOUT LAUGHTER."
E.E. CUMMINGS

Are you uptight about life or do you
see the humor each day brings?

_____

_____

_____

_____

_____

_____

MAY 18

"TELL PEOPLE WHAT YOU LOVE
ABOUT THEM. LESS CRITICISM,
MORE COMPLIMENTS."
LORI DESCHENE

The news is addicted to drama and trauma as humans are drawn to gossip. How can you genuinely compliment someone every day to uplift their mind and spirit?

_____

_____

_____

_____

_____

MAY 19

"FAILURE IS ALWAYS A BLESSING
WHEN IT FORCES ONE TO ACQUIRE
KNOWLEDGE OR TO BUILD HABITS
THAT LEAD TO THE ACHIEVEMENT
OF ONE'S MAJOR PURPOSE IN LIFE."
NAPOLEON HILL

What's a recent setback that taught
you a good lesson that ultimately
helped improve your life?

MAY 20

"IT'S A FUNNY THING ABOUT LIFE, ONCE YOU BEGIN TO TAKE NOTE OF THE THINGS YOU ARE GRATEFUL FOR, YOU BEGIN TO LOSE SIGHT OF THE THINGS YOU LACK." GERMANY KENT

Do you look for the good in every day, or do you often find fault with yourself and the thoughts you think?

MAY 21

"DISCIPLINE IS THE PATHWAY TO
FREEDOM."
JOCKO WILLINK

Are your good habits outweighing the
challenging ones? Explain.

MAY 22

"BE COOL TO PEOPLE. BE NICE
TO AS MANY PEOPLE AS YOU
CAN. SMILE TO AS MANY PEOPLE
AS YOU CAN, AND HAVE THEM
SMILE BACK AT YOU."
JOE ROGAN

Who are three people today you can
send a positive text, comment, call, or
smile?

_____

_____

_____

_____

_____

_____

MAY 23

"LEARN TO BE THANKFUL FOR
WHAT YOU ALREADY HAVE,
WHILE YOU PURSUE ALL THAT
YOU WANT."
JIM ROHN

Are you looking too far ahead and
failing to see the good in each day as
it happens?

_____

_____

_____

_____

_____

_____

MAY 24

"RIGHT NOW, YOU ARE THE
CONSEQUENCE OF OTHER
PEOPLE'S OPINIONS ABOUT YOU.
WHY GIVE ANYONE THAT MUCH
POWER OR CONTROL OVER YOU?"
SADHGURU

Do you find yourself trying to people-
please others, or do you consider
yourself an independent thinker?

_____

_____

_____

_____

_____

_____

MAY 25

"LESSONS IN LIFE WILL BE
REPEATED UNTIL THEY ARE
LEARNED."
FRANK SONNENBERG

Which area of your life or business
continues to be a problem? How can
you look at it from a different angle?

MAY 26

"JUDGE A MAN BY HIS
QUESTIONS RATHER THAN BY HIS
ANSWERS."
VOLTAIRE

Are you in a continual state of learning or do are you stuck in a rut?

MAY 27

"IN THE MIDST OF CHAOS, THERE IS ALSO OPPORTUNITY."
SUN TZU

What area in your life is chaotic and not up to par, that if addressed, would improve it?

_____

_____

_____

_____

_____

_____

MAY 28

"I FOUND OUT THAT THERE
WEREN'T TOO MANY
LIMITATIONS, IF I DID IT MY
WAY."
JOHNNY CASH

Where do you find yourself limited?
How can you change to lessen it?

_____

_____

_____

_____

_____

_____

MAY 29

"ENLIGHTEN THE PEOPLE
GENERALLY, AND TYRANNY, AND
OPPRESSIONS OF BODY AND MIND
WILL VANISH LIKE EVIL SPIRITS
AT THE DAWN OF DAY."
THOMAS JEFFERSON

What are you doing each day to grow,
learn, mentor others, and push
yourself forward?

MAY 30

"A NEW DAY, A NEW PAGE, THE
CHANCE TO WRITE YOUR LIFE
THE WAY YOU WANT IT TO BE."
KAREN AREL

What can you do to treat today like a
brand new blank page full of
possibility?

MAY 31

"LEADERSHIP, ON THE OTHER
HAND, IS ABOUT CREATING
CHANGE YOU BELIEVE IN."
SETH GODIN

What idea or suggestion do you need
to pitch to create the change you want
to see?

_____

_____

_____

_____

_____

_____

JUNE

JUNE 1

"LOOK AT LIFE THROUGH THE
WINDSHIELD, NOT THE REAR-
VIEW MIRROR."
BYRD BAGGETT

Are you more forward-looking with
life, or do you find yourself
constantly looking to the past?

_____

_____

_____

_____

_____

_____

JUNE 2

"THERE ARE THOSE WHO CAN
AND THOSE WHO DO; BE VERY
CAREFUL WHO YOU LISTEN TO."
MARK GLEASON

Who are you getting advice from and
do they have your genuine interest in
mind?

_____

_____

_____

_____

_____

_____

JUNE 3

"PERFECTION IS ANOTHER FORM
OF PROCRASTINATION."
TOM SMOLINSKI

Are you good at making excuses as to why your life isn't better than what it truly could be? What do you need to do to create action?

_____

_____

_____

_____

_____

JUNE 4

"SUCCESS IS NOT A PLACE AT
WHICH ONE ARRIVES, BUT
RATHER THE SPIRIT WITH WHICH
ONE UNDERTAKES AND
CONTINUES THE JOURNEY."
ALEX NOBLE

What does success look like to you?

_____

_____

_____

_____

_____

_____

JUNE 5

"FINDING OUR TRUE CALLING IN LIFE IS NOT AN EASY TASK. NO MATTER WHAT PHASE OF LIFE WE ARE IN, THERE ARE PRESSURES TO CONFORM TO A PARTICULAR STANDARD. AS WE PLOW THROUGH OUR DAYS, WE MUST ALL KEEP ASKING: WHAT DO I REALLY WANT TO DO IN LIFE?" J.R. GORK

What do you really want to do in life?

_____

_____

_____

_____

_____

_____

JUNE 6

"A COINCIDENCE IS A MIRACLE IN
WHICH GOD WISHES TO REMAIN
ANONYMOUS."
ANONYMOUS

What coincidence in your life turned
out to be a miracle?

_____

_____

_____

_____

_____

_____

JUNE 7

"DON'T TELL PEOPLE YOUR
PLANS. SHOW THEM YOUR
RESULTS."
UNKNOWN

What actions are you taking today to
create results that advance you toward
your life goals?

_____

_____

_____

_____

_____

_____

JUNE 8

"WHEN YOU'RE SCARED BUT STILL DO IT ANYWAY, THAT'S BRAVE."
NEIL GAIMEN

What can you do today to demonstrate bravery?

_____

_____

_____

_____

_____

_____

JUNE 9

"BE FEARLESS IN THE PURSUIT OF
WHAT SETS YOUR SOUL ON FIRE."
JENNIFER LEE

What are you pursuing right now that
makes you come alive when you talk
about or do it?

_____

_____

_____

_____

_____

_____

JUNE 10

"PEOPLE WORRY SO MUCH ABOUT
THE COST OF LIVING. CONCERN
YOURSELF WITH THE VALUE OF
LIFE."
HANK MOORE

Do you constantly look at the price of
everything versus the value it will
bring to your life? Explain.

_____

_____

_____

_____

_____

_____

JUNE 11

"START THE DAY WITH A
GRATEFUL HEART."
TINA HARNISH JOHNSON

How are you setting up each day for
gratitude and success?

_____

_____

_____

_____

_____

_____

JUNE 12

"EVERY SAINT HAS A PAST AND
EVERY SINNER HAS A FUTURE."
OSCAR WILDE

What past mistake do you need to let
go of and free yourself of so you can
positively move ahead?

_____

_____

_____

_____

_____

_____

JUNE 13

"THE BEST THING ABOUT THE
FUTURE IS THAT IT COMES ONE
DAY AT A TIME."
ABE LINCOLN

Are you enjoying the present moment
more than the future, which isn't
guaranteed? Explain.

_____

_____

_____

_____

_____

_____

JUNE 14

"THE LAST RESULT OF WISDOM
STAMPS IT TRUE; HE ONLY EARNS
HIS FREEDOM AND EXISTENCE,
WHO DAILY CONQUERS THEM
ANEW."
GOETHE

Are you growing or stagnating?
Explain.

JUNE 15

"IN RECOGNIZING THE HUMANITY OF OUR FELLOW BEINGS, WE PAY OURSELVES THE HIGHEST TRIBUTE."
THURGOOD MARSHALL

Are you empathetic toward and accepting of others who are different than you? Explain.

_____

_____

_____

_____

_____

_____

JUNE 16

"WHEN YOU THINK A THOUGHT THAT RINGS TRUE WITH WHO YOU REALLY ARE, YOU FEEL HARMONY COURSING THROUGH YOUR PHYSICAL BODY: JOY, LOVE, AND A SENSE OF FREEDOM ARE EXAMPLES OF THAT ALIGNMENT." ESTHER HICKS

Are you feeling harmony within your life and relationships? Explain.

_____

_____

_____

_____

_____

_____

JUNE 17

"EVEN DURING A SHIPWRECK,
SOMEONE HAS TO ROW THE
BOAT."
ERIC REUSCH

Are you a leader or a follower when
fear or chaos strikes?

_____

_____

_____

_____

_____

_____

JUNE 18

"LIVE YOUR DREAMS AND BELIEVE
IN YOURSELF; THAT IS THE ONLY
WAY TO THE TOP."
ANDY LAPOINTE

Do you trust your own talents and
passions? Explain.

_____

_____

_____

_____

_____

_____

JUNE 19

"HAPPINESS STARTS FROM
WITHIN AND GROWS OUTWARD."
TONY RUBLESKI

Do you listen to your own ideas,
intuition, and prayers for inspiration
and joy?

JUNE 20

"FAMILY IS NOT AN IMPORTANT
THING. IT'S EVERYTHING."
MICHAEL J. FOX

Do you value your family and what
role does it play in your life?

_____

_____

_____

_____

_____

_____

JUNE 21

"FAILURE BRINGS A CLIMAX IN
WHICH ONE HAS THE PRIVILEGE
OF CLEARING HIS MIND OF FEAR
AND MAKING A NEW START IN
ANOTHER DIRECTION."
NAPOLEON HILL

What fear in your life allowed you
freedom to start anew and find
success elsewhere?

_____

_____

_____

_____

_____

_____

JUNE 22

"IF YOU ARE ALWAYS TRYING TO BE NORMAL YOU WILL NEVER KNOW HOW AMAZING YOU CAN BE."
MAYA ANGELOU

When's the last time you pushed your comfort zone and tried something new?

JUNE 23

"THE MAN WHO MOVES A
MOUNTAIN BEGINS BY CARRYING
AWAY SMALL STONES."
CONFUCIUS

How can you break down a big goal or
project into smaller, daily steps?

JUNE 24

"WHAT YOU DO SPEAKS SO
LOUDLY THAT I CANNOT HEAR
WHAT YOU SAY."
RALPH WALDO EMERSON

Are you consistent with your words
and actions, or do you fail to "walk
the talk?"

JUNE 25

"STRESS, ANXIETY, AND DEPRESSION ARE CAUSED WHEN WE ARE LIVING TO PLEASE OTHERS."
PAULO COELHO

Do you truly enjoy your work or calling, or is it something you want to consider changing to find greater joy and satisfaction?

JUNE 26

"A CREATIVE MAN IS MOTIVATED
BY THE DESIRE TO ACHIEVE, NOT
BY THE DESIRE TO BEAT
OTHERS."
AYN RAND

Do you compete with yourself to
improve each day, or to show-up
others?

JUNE 27

"BEAUTY IS NOT IN THE FACE;
BEAUTY IS A LIGHT IN THE
HEART."
KAHLIL GIBRAN

Do you see the uniqueness and beauty
in others that are different from you?

JUNE 28

"ANXIETY WEIGHS DOWN THE
HEART, BUT A KIND WORD
CHEERS IT UP."
PROVERBS 12:25

What's your favorite book, podcast,
song, movie, quote, prayer, person or
memory that lifts you up when feeling
down?

JUNE 29

"IF YOU DON'T STOP TO SMELL
THE ROSES NOW, THEY MIGHT
END UP ON YOU."
BOB MOULD

When's the last time you slowed
down, without distraction, to take in
the beauty of this world?

JUNE 30

"EVEN IN THE FACE OF TRAGEDY,
A STELLAR PERSON CAN THRIVE.
NO MATTER WHAT'S GOING ON IN
YOUR LIFE, YOU CAN OVERCOME
IT."
KEANU REEVES

What setback in your life did you
work through where you got better,
not bitter?

_____

_____

_____

_____

_____

_____

JULY

JULY 1

"NO ACT OF KINDNESS, NO MATTER HOW SMALL, IS EVER WASTED."
AESOP

What's a random act of kindness you can perform today for someone you know or for a complete stranger?

_____

_____

_____

_____

_____

_____

JULY 2

"WHEN YOU WANT SOMETHING,
YOU HAVE TO BE WILLING TO
PAY YOUR DUES."
LES BROWN

What unfinished goal do you need to focus on again and make a priority to complete?

_____

_____

_____

_____

_____

_____

JULY 3

"A GEM CANNOT BE POLISHED
WITHOUT FRICTION, NOR A MAN
PERFECTED WITHOUT TRIALS."
SENECA

What is a major trial you faced that
you came out better after going
through it?

JULY 4

"COURAGE IS BEING SCARED TO
DEATH, BUT SADDLING UP
ANYWAY."
JOHN WAYNE

What big fear do you need to look at
addressing right now versus delaying
it another day?

JULY 5

"VISION WITHOUT EXECUTION IS
HALLUCINATION."
THOMAS EDISON

What idea, goal, or dream do you
need to start taking action towards?

_____

_____

_____

_____

_____

_____

JULY 6

"LIFE ISN'T ABOUT GETTING AND
HAVING, IT'S ABOUT GIVING AND
BEING."
KEVIN KRUSE

What act of kindness can you freely
give to someone you meet today?

_____

_____

_____

_____

_____

_____

JULY 7

"IF YOU WANT TO LIFT
SOMEBODY ELSE UP, LIFT UP
YOURSELF."
BOOKER T. WASHINGTON

What will you do today to strengthen
and renew your body, mind, and
spirit?

_____

_____

_____

_____

_____

_____

JULY 8

"WHEN WE ARE NO LONGER ABLE
TO CHANGE A SITUATION, WE
ARE CHALLENGED TO CHANGE
OURSELVES."
VIKTOR FRANKL

What area in your life feels stuck and
what action can you take to change it?

JULY 9

"WITH THE EXCEPTION OF WISDOM, I'M INCLINED TO BELIEVE THAT THE IMMORTAL GODS HAVE GIVEN NOTHING BETTER TO HUMANITY THAN FRIENDSHIP." CICERO

List your top three friends, how long you've known them, and what you value most about them.

_____

_____

_____

_____

_____

_____

JULY 10

"THE ONLY THING WORSE THAN
BEING BLIND IS HAVING SIGHT
BUT NO VISION."
HELEN KELLER

Do you feel like a key area within
your life is stuck and how can you
work at seeing it from a different
perspective?

JULY 11

"YOU'VE GOT TO ASK. ASKING IS,
IN MY OPINION, THE WORLD'S
MOST POWERFUL AND
NEGLECTED SECRET TO SUCCESS
AND HAPPINESS."
PERCY ROSS

What area of life do you need to ask
more from before your head hits the
pillow tonight?

JULY 12

"NO MATTER WHAT PEOPLE TELL
YOU, WORDS AND IDEAS CAN
CHANGE THE WORLD."
ROBIN WILLIAMS

What's an idea you've had in your
mind that gets you excited? Have you
been procrastinating and if so why? If
you're taking action toward it,
explain.

_____

_____

_____

_____

_____

JULY 13

"THERE IS NO PRACTICE MORE DEGRADING, DEBASING, AND SOUL DESTROYING THAN THAT OF SELF-PITY. CAST IT OUT FROM YOU."
JAMES ALLEN

What grievance are you still carrying in your head that you need to finally let go of?

_____

_____

_____

_____

_____

_____

JULY 14

"IF YOUR ACTIONS INSPIRE OTHERS TO DREAM MORE, LEARN MORE, AND BECOME MORE, YOU ARE A LEADER."
JOHN QUINCY ADAMS

Are you leading others? How are you being—or could you be—a good leader?

_____

_____

_____

_____

_____

_____

JULY 15

"PEOPLE WILL COME AND GO IN
YOUR LIFE. HOWEVER, THE
WISDOM AND LESSONS THEY
SHARE WILL NEVER LEAVE YOU."
TONY RUBLESKI

Do you let unwise emotions or anger
cloud your ability to see the lessons
from people in your current or past
life? How can you focus on the
lessons versus the experiences more?

JULY 16

"NO ONE IS USELESS IN THIS
WORLD WHO LIGHTENS THE
BURDENS OF ANOTHER."
CHARLES DICKENS

The world is loaded with critics and complainers. What can you do today to not join them?

JULY 17

"AS I GROW OLDER, I PAY LESS
ATTENTION TO WHAT MEN SAY. I
JUST WATCH WHAT THEY DO."
ANDREW CARNEGIE

Are your actions showing consistency
with your words? How can you
practice what you preach more?

_____

_____

_____

_____

_____

_____

JULY 18

"LOVING MEANS SHARING JOY
WITH PEOPLE."
LEO BUSCAGLIA

Are you lifting people up each day and sharing in their joys, or are you holding back out of fear, jealousy, or pride?

JULY 19

"ANYONE WHO ATTEMPTS TO
BUILD GREAT THINGS WILL FACE
CHALLENGES."
JON GORDON

Are you willing to persist and not
quit on your goals at the first signs of
resistance? What plan have you
created to help you persist when you
face challenges?

_____

_____

_____

_____

_____

JULY 20

"HAPPINESS IS THE NEW RICH. INNER PEACE IS THE NEW SUCCESS. HEALTH IS THE NEW WEALTH. KINDNESS IS THE NEW COOL."
SYED BALKHI

Are you chasing the wrong things in life and feeling deep down unfulfilled? If yes, what needs to change?

_____

_____

_____

_____

_____

_____

JULY 21

"A WINNER IS A DREAMER WHO
NEVER GIVES UP."
NELSON MANDELA

When's the last time you dreamed and
took immediate action on it?

_____

_____

_____

_____

_____

_____

JULY 22

"NEVER COMPLAIN. NEVER
EXPLAIN."
KATHERINE HEPBURN

People deep down have little patience
for those who complain. Are you
complaining too much or are you
finding healthy ways to handle stress
and fears?

_____

_____

_____

_____

_____

JULY 23

"IF YOU DON'T LOVE YOURSELF
YOU'LL NEVER FEEL LIKE ANYONE
ELSE DOES EITHER."
BRIDGETT DEVOUE

Do you truly love yourself? Are you
taking care of yourself each day or
are you running on fumes trying to
make everyone else happy?

JULY 24

"YOUR BODY CANNOT HEAL
WITHOUT PLAY. YOUR MIND
CANNOT HEAL WITHOUT
LAUGHTER. YOUR SOUL CANNOT
HEAL WITHOUT JOY."
CATHERINE FENWICK

How do you add more play, laughter,
and joy into your daily life?

JULY 25

"WE DON'T STOP PLAYING
BECAUSE WE GROW OLD; WE
GROW OLD BECAUSE WE STOP
PLAYING."
GEORGE BERNARD SHAW

When's the last time you played or
participated in a game and had a lot
of fun? How can you incorporate play
into your life more often?

JULY 26

"EVEN IN A WORLD THAT'S BEING
SHIPWRECKED, REMAIN BRAVE
AND STRONG."
HILDEGARD OF BINGEN

How do you stay strong and
consistent with your thoughts and
actions when people or things around
you may be falling apart?

JULY 27

"NONE ARE SO EMPTY AS THOSE
WHO ARE FULL OF THEMSELVES."
ANDREW JACKSON

Are you confident, not cocky, and do
you truly listen to others instead of
just to yourself?

_____

_____

_____

_____

_____

_____

JULY 28

"S.T.R.E.S.S. = SOMEONE TRYING
TO REPAIR EVERY SITUATION
SOLO."
DAVE WILLIS

Are you the Lone Ranger or do you
have a good team to turn to and help
you when needed?

JULY 29

"YOU CAN GET EVERYTHING IN LIFE YOU WANT IF YOU WILL JUST HELP ENOUGH OTHER PEOPLE GET WHAT THEY WANT."
ZIG ZIGLAR

Do you silently keep score with others, or do you give with love and no strings attached?

_____

_____

_____

_____

_____

_____

JULY 30

"GIVING OPENS THE WAY FOR
RECEIVING."
FLORENCE SHINN

Giving is a universal law. Are you
flowing with or resisting it?

_____

_____

_____

_____

_____

_____

JULY 31

"ANGRY PEOPLE WANT TO SEE HOW POWERFUL THEY ARE. LOVING PEOPLE WANT YOU TO SEE HOW POWERFUL YOU ARE."
CHIEF RED EAGLE

What can you do today to lift someone up and encourage them to improve?

_____

_____

_____

_____

_____

_____

AUGUST

AUGUST 1

"TOO MANY PEOPLE SPEND
MONEY THEY HAVEN'T EARNED,
TO BUY THINGS THEY DON'T
WANT, TO IMPRESS PEOPLE THEY
DON'T LIKE."
WILL ROGERS

Are you trying too hard to impress
others by "keeping up with the
Joneses" or are you being true to
yourself?

_____

_____

_____

_____

_____

_____

AUGUST 2

"IF YOU DON'T LEARN TO LAUGH
AT TROUBLE, YOU WON'T HAVE
ANYTHING TO LAUGH AT WHEN
YOU'RE OLD."
E.W. HOWE

What's a situation in your past, that
at the time was bad or super stressful,
that you can look back on now with
laughter?

_____

_____

_____

_____

_____

AUGUST 3

"LIFE BECOMES EASIER WHEN
YOU LEARN TO ACCEPT THE
APOLOGY YOU NEVER GOT."
R. BRAULT

What person or action do you still
hold resentment toward that you need
to finally forgive and move on from?

_____

_____

_____

_____

_____

_____

AUGUST 4

"EVERYONE WANTS TO LIVE ON
TOP OF THE MOUNTAIN, BUT ALL
THE HAPPINESS AND GROWTH
OCCURS WHILE YOU'RE CLIMBING
IT."
ANDY ROONEY

Are you living in the future more than
the present? How can you enjoy the
"climb" more?

AUGUST 5

"BEAUTY BEGINS THE MOMENT
YOU DECIDE TO BE YOURSELF."
COCO CHANEL

How long has it been since you
looked in the mirror and realized how
incredible and unique you truly are?

_____

_____

_____

_____

_____

_____

AUGUST 6

"NO VALID PLANS FOR THE
FUTURE CAN BE MADE BY THOSE
WHO HAVE NO CAPACITY FOR
LIVING NOW."
ALAN WATTS

Do you live each day with optimism
and faith, or do you look backward or
forward more than you should?

AUGUST 7

"HAVE THE MATURITY TO KNOW
SOMETIMES SILENCE IS MORE
POWERFUL THAN HAVING THE
LAST WORD."
THEMA DAVIS

Is your peace of mind more important
to you than your pride?

_____

_____

_____

_____

_____

_____

AUGUST 8

"WHERE THERE IS FEAR, WORRY,
ANXIETY, DOUBT, AND TROUBLE,
THERE IS IGNORANCE AND LACK
OF FAITH."
JAMES ALLEN

If a positive attitude is key to a happy
life, what are you doing today to
ensure that negativity and fear is kept
in check?

AUGUST 9

"SHOWING OFF IS THE FOOL'S
IDEA OF GLORY."
BRUCE LEE

In the world of social media, are you being yourself or are you trying too hard to show off to others by excessive posting or sharing?

AUGUST 10

"OUR GREATEST WEAPON
AGAINST STRESS IS OUR ABILITY
TO CHOOSE ONE THOUGHT OVER
ANOTHER."
WILLIAM JAMES

Do you control your mind to stay
focused, or do you often react out of
fear and worry?

_____

_____

_____

_____

_____

_____

AUGUST 11

"MAKE EACH DAY YOUR
MASTERPIECE."
JOHN WOODEN

If this was your last day alive, what
would you do before the clock struck
midnight?

_____

_____

_____

_____

_____

_____

AUGUST 12

"LOVE IS THE ONLY FREEDOM
FROM ATTACHMENT. WHEN YOU
LOVE EVERYTHING, YOU ARE
ATTACHED TO NOTHING."
MIKHAIL NAIMY

Who or what are you clinging to right
now that needs to be released?

_____

_____

_____

_____

_____

_____

AUGUST 13

"HAPPINESS CAN BE FOUND,
EVEN IN THE DARKEST OF TIMES,
IF ONE ONLY REMEMBERS TO
TURN ON THE LIGHT."
DUMBLEDORE*

Write down five things that you are deeply grateful for in your life at this present moment.

_____

_____

_____

_____

_____

Harry Potter and the Prisoner of Azkaban, from the screenplay by Steven Kloves.

AUGUST 14

"IN ANY GIVEN MOMENT WE
HAVE TWO OPTIONS: TO STEP
FORWARD INTO GROWTH OR TO
STEP BACK INTO SAFETY."
ABRAHAM MASLOW

Are you coasting in life right now or
are pushing yourself to get better?

AUGUST 15

"EACH DAY IS A GIFT, NOT A GRIND."
TONY RUBLESKI

Do you consistently wake up with gratitude and anticipation or do you find yourself bored and uninspired by life?

AUGUST 16

"FEAR MAKES THE WOLF BIGGER
THAN HE IS."
GERMAN PROVERB

What fear have you conquered in your
life that taught you a positive lesson?

AUGUST 17

"LEARN HOW TO TURN FRUSTRATION
INTO FASCINATION. YOU WILL
LEARN MORE BEING FASCINATED BY
LIFE THAN YOU WILL BY BEING
FRUSTRATED BY IT."
JIM ROHN

What situation in your past or present
that upset you can you view as a
lesson and not a setback?

_____

_____

_____

_____

_____

_____

AUGUST 18

"IN SCHOOL, YOU'RE TAUGHT A
LESSON AND THEN GIVEN A TEST.
IN LIFE, YOU'RE GIVEN A TEST
THAT TEACHES YOU A LESSON."
TOM BODETT

Explain a recent life test than you
endured and what you learned from
it?

AUGUST 19

"THE ONLY REAL ANTIDOTE FOR
WORRY IS ACTION."
DAN S. KENNEDY

What's one positive thing you can do
today to start addressing a big issue
you're currently facing?

AUGUST 20

"IF YOU WANT TOTAL SECURITY,
GO TO PRISON. THERE YOU'RE
FED, CLOTHED, GIVEN MEDICAL
CARE AND SO ON. THE ONLY
THING LACKING...IS FREEDOM."
DWIGHT D. EISENHOWER

How can you enjoy and appreciate
today and the freedoms provided to
you?

AUGUST 21

"WHAT YOU LEAVE BEHIND IS
NOT WHAT IS ENGRAVED IN
STONE MONUMENTS, BUT WHAT
IS WOVEN INTO THE LIVES OF
OTHERS."
PERICLES

Who is a person you can share a kind
word, compliment, or message with
today?

_____

_____

_____

_____

_____

_____

AUGUST 22

"LIFE IS SHORT, BREAK THE
RULES. KISS SLOWLY. LOVE
TRULY. LAUGH UNCONTROLLABLY
AND NEVER REGRET ANYTHING
THAT MAKES YOU SMILE."
MARK TWAIN

What can you do today that will make
you smile and glad to be alive?

_____

_____

_____

_____

_____

_____

AUGUST 23

"OUR GREATEST GLORY IS NOT IN
NEVER FALLING, BUT IN RISING
EVERY TIME WE FALL."
CONFUCIUS

When you fall, how do you pick
yourself back up?

_____

_____

_____

_____

_____

_____

AUGUST 24

"FIND JOY IN THE ORDINARY."
MAX LUCADO

Are you present and enjoying each part of your days, or do you often find yourself skipping ahead to the future?

AUGUST 25

"TO AVOID CRITICISM, DO
NOTHING, SAY NOTHING, AND BE
NOTHING."
ELBERT HUBBARD

Are you playing it too safe and
conservative with your life, talents,
and ideas? Explain.

_____

_____

_____

_____

_____

_____

AUGUST 26

"SUCCESS AND ALL GOOD THINGS
IN LIFE, START WITH A GENUINE
CONCERN FOR OTHERS."
MIKE VANCE

Who need to receive a checkup call,
visit, or text from you today?

AUGUST 27

"FOLLOW YOUR PASSIONS,
BELIEVE IN KARMA, AND YOU
WON'T HAVE TO CHASE YOUR
DREAMS, THEY WILL COME TO
YOU."
RANDY PAUSCH

What do you really enjoy that needs
to be given more priority within your
life?

AUGUST 28

"INNOVATION DISTINGUISHES
BETWEEN A LEADER AND A
FOLLOWER."
STEVE JOBS

How can you be more innovative and
confident with your own ideas?

"CHOOSE YOUR FRIENDS WITH
CAUTION. PLAN YOUR FUTURE
WITH PURPOSE. FRAME YOUR LIFE
WITH FAITH."
THOMAS MONSON

Is your immediate circle of friends
uplifting and supportive, or are they
often negative and pessimistic?

AUGUST 30

"EVERYTHING YOU'VE EVER
WANTED IS ON THE OTHER SIDE
OF FEAR."
GEORGE ADAIR

When's the last time you took a risk
in your life that turned out better than
you could've possibly imagined?

AUGUST 31

"YOUR ASSUMPTIONS ARE YOUR
WINDOWS OF THE WORLD. SCRUB
THEM OFF EVERY ONCE IN A
WHILE, OR THE LIGHT WON'T
COME IN."
ISAAC ASIMOV

What idea or belief do you cling to
that needs a deep review or scrubbing
to see if it still serves you well?

_____

_____

_____

_____

_____

_____

SEPTEMBER

SEPTEMBER 1

"A BAD ATTITUDE IS LIKE A FLAT
TIRE. YOU CAN'T GO ANYWHERE
UNTIL YOU CHANGE IT."
EARL NIGHTINGALE

Is your self-talk more positive than
negative? How can you practice
positive self-talk?

_____

_____

_____

_____

_____

_____

SEPTEMBER 2

"IF YOU WANT TO LIVE A HAPPY
LIFE, TIE IT TO A GOAL, NOT TO
PEOPLE OR OBJECTS."
ALBERT EINSTEIN

What goal in your life gets you up
early and keeps you up late?

SEPTEMBER 3

"WHEN 99% OF PEOPLE DOUBT
YOU, YOU'RE EITHER GRAVELY
WRONG OR ABOUT TO MAKE
HISTORY."
TIM FERRISS

When's the last time you tried
something new that had your friends
and family say, "No way! Are you
kidding?"

SEPTEMBER 4

"FIND A PLACE INSIDE WHERE
THERE'S JOY, AND THE JOY WILL
BURN OUT THE PAIN."
JOSEPH CAMPBELL

When you have a bad moment or day,
what do you do to snap out of it and
shift your mindset to the better?

_____

_____

_____

_____

_____

_____

SEPTEMBER 5

"BEING HONEST MAY NOT GET
YOU A LOT OF FRIENDS, BUT
IT'LL ALWAYS GET YOU THE
RIGHT ONES."
JOHN LENNON

Who in your circle loves you enough
to share advice that you don't always
want to hear?

SEPTEMBER 6

"COMPANIES THRIVE ON THE
BASIS OF THE STORIES THEY
TELL."
JAY ABRAHAM

What core story drives you to pursue
your passion or career?

SEPTEMBER 7

"I HAVE FAR MORE RESPECT FOR
THE PERSON WITH A SINGLE IDEA
WHO GETS THERE, THAN FOR THE
PERSON WITH A THOUSAND IDEAS
WHO DOES NOTHING."
THOMAS EDISON

What big idea or project do you need
to take action on starting today?

_____

_____

_____

_____

_____

_____

SEPTEMBER 8

"PEOPLE MAY HEAR YOUR
WORDS, BUT THEY FEEL YOUR
ATTITUDE."
JOHN MAXWELL

Do you walk the talk, or do you find
yourself going back and wavering on
your commitments?

SEPTEMBER 9

"TALKING ABOUT OUR PROBLEMS
IS OUR GREATEST ADDICTION.
BREAK THE HABIT. TALK ABOUT
YOUR JOYS."
RITA SCHIANO

Listen to yourself. Do you talk more
about the positive things happening in
your life or problems and worries?

SEPTEMBER 10

"SHIPS IN HARBOR ARE SAFE, BUT
THAT'S NOT WHAT SHIPS ARE
BUILT FOR."
JOHN SHEDD

What in your life have you been
putting off for far too long and not
acting on and why?

SEPTEMBER 11

"JUST BECAUSE YOU ARE
DIFFERENT DOES NOT MEAN
THAT YOU HAVE TO BE
REJECTED."
EARTHA KITT

Do you celebrate or hide your uniqueness?

_____

_____

_____

_____

_____

_____

SEPTEMBER 12

"WHEN YOU BELIEVE, YOUR MIND
WILL FIND A WAY."
DAVID J. SCHWARTZ

Do you believe in your own gifts and
talents, or do you wait for others to
approve?

_____

_____

_____

_____

_____

_____

SEPTEMBER 13

"EACH PERSON MUST LIVE THEIR LIFE AS A MODEL FOR OTHERS."
ROSA PARKS

Who are you trying to set a good example for?

_____

_____

_____

_____

_____

_____

SEPTEMBER 14

"IF YOU HAVE GOOD THOUGHTS
THEY WILL SHINE OUT OF YOUR
FACE LIKE SUNBEAMS AND YOU
WILL ALWAYS LOOK LOVELY."
ROALD DAHL

Do people feel good in your presence?

_____

_____

_____

_____

_____

_____

SEPTEMBER 15

"POSITIVE DISRUPTION IS THE
NEW NORMAL. PLAYING-IT-SAFE
IS THE PATH TO MEDIOCRITY."
TONY RUBLESKI

How do you create and implement
positive new actions and ideas into
your life?

_____

_____

_____

_____

_____

_____

_____

SEPTEMBER 16

"YOUR PROBLEM IS YOU'RE TOO
BUSY HOLDING ONTO YOUR
UNWORTHINESS."
RAM DASS

What negative belief do you need to
let go of that is not serving you well?

SEPTEMBER 17

"BUT I ALWAYS THINK THAT THE
BEST WAY TO KNOW GOD IS TO
LOVE MANY THINGS."
VINCENT VAN GOGH

Are you a creature of habit, or do you
make it a goal to push yourself to
learn, grow, discover new things, and
meet new people?

SEPTEMBER 18

"LIVE, SO YOU DO NOT HAVE TO
LOOK BACK AND SAY: GOD, HOW
I HAVE WASTED MY LIFE."
ELISABETH KUBLER-ROSS

Are you moving forward in life, or do
you feel stuck with excuses and
denial?

SEPTEMBER 19

"A MAN OF COURAGE IS ALSO
FULL OF FAITH."
CICERO

Do you go it alone or have faith in a
higher power?

_____

_____

_____

_____

_____

_____

SEPTEMBER 20

"THE HARDER THE CONFLICT,
THE MORE GLORIOUS THE
TRIUMPH."
THOMAS PAINE

When's the last time you really pushed hard to knock out a goal or tough project when facing intense criticism and doubt?

SEPTEMBER 21

"IT IS NOT UNCOMMON FOR
PEOPLE TO SPEND THEIR WHOLE
LIFE WAITING TO START LIVING."
ECKHART TOLLE

What area in your life do you feel
like you're wasting time that needs to
be changed?

SEPTEMBER 22

"FEEL THE FEELING BUT DON'T BECOME THE EMOTION. WITNESS IT. ALLOW IT. RELEASE IT."
CRYSTAL ANDRUS

Are you a slave to your emotions, compulsions, and internal drama, or do you step back, take a hard look and let them go?

SEPTEMBER 23

"I LOVE TO LAUGH, I LOVE THE
JOY OF LIFE, AND I LOVE
SHARING IT."
CHITA RIVERA

What do you love about your life
right now?

SEPTEMBER 24

"LIFE IS NOT A MATTER OF
HOLDING GOOD CARDS, BUT
SOMETIMES, PLAYING A POOR
HAND WELL."
JACK LONDON

Do you let setbacks delay you or
create excessive doubt, or do you
quickly adapt, improvise, and keep
moving forward?

SEPTEMBER 25

"YOU SIMPLY HAVE TO PUT ONE FOOT IN FRONT OF THE OTHER AND KEEP GOING. PUT BLINDERS ON AND PLOW RIGHT AHEAD."
GEORGE LUCAS

How do you put blinders on and move forward when facing frustration, doubt or criticism?

_____

_____

_____

_____

_____

_____

_____

SEPTEMBER 26

"SOME PEOPLE DIE AT 25 AND
AREN'T BURIED UNTIL 75."
BEN FRANKLIN

Are you stuck in a rut and taking life
for granted?

_____

_____

_____

_____

_____

_____

"NO MATTER WHO YOU ARE,
WE'RE CREATURES OF HABIT. THE
BETTER YOUR HABITS ARE, THE
BETTER THEY WILL BE IN
PRESSURE SITUATIONS."
WAYNE GRETZKY

What positive new habit could you
add into your life that would pay
multiple dividends if you made it a
priority?

_____

_____

_____

_____

_____

_____

SEPTEMBER 28

"YOU'LL NEVER CHANGE THE
WORLD IF YOU'RE WORRIED
ABOUT BEING LIKED."
ROBIN SHARMA

Do you worry too much about being
liked instead of standing up for what
you believe in?

_____

_____

_____

_____

_____

_____

SEPTEMBER 29

"IT IS THOSE WHO CONCENTRATE
ON BUT ONE THING AT A TIME
WHO ADVANCE IN THIS WORLD."
OG MANDINO

Do you use distraction, work, people,
or lack of discipline as an excuse to
delay or not complete goals, projects,
or commitments with others?

SEPTEMBER 30

"IT'S TIME TO STOP LETTING
YOUR HISTORY CONTROL YOUR
DESTINY."
ANDY ANDREWS

What experience or person do you
need to let go of today?

_____

_____

_____

_____

_____

_____

OCTOBER

OCTOBER 1

"BE THE PERSON THAT WHEN
YOUR FEET TOUCH THE FLOOR IN
THE MORNING THE DEVIL SAYS,
"AWE SHIT. THEY'RE UP."
THE ROCK

Do you get up each day with a goal or
mission to inspire and push you
forward?

OCTOBER 2

"WHEN YOU CHANGE YOUR
ENERGY, YOU CHANGE YOUR
LIFE."
DR. JOE DISPENZA

Do you approach most days with
positive energy or do you complain
and focus on the negatives?

OCTOBER 3

"LIFE IS CONTINUOUSLY
CHANGING, AND IF YOU'RE
TRYING TO CONTROL IT, YOU'LL
NEVER BE ABLE TO FULLY LIVE
IT."
MICHAEL SINGER

What is a daily concern of yours that
you need to change, drop, or rethink
to produce greater happiness?

_____

_____

_____

_____

_____

OCTOBER 4

"QUICKNESS IS THE ESSENCE
OF WAR."
SUN TZU

Do you let opportunities pass you by
due to overthinking?

OCTOBER 5

"PEOPLE WON'T HAVE TIME FOR
YOU IF YOU ARE ALWAYS ANGRY
OR COMPLAINING."
STEPHEN HAWKING

Are people drawn to you or are you
too guarded or skeptical?

_____

_____

_____

_____

_____

_____

OCTOBER 6

"INTEGRITY IS EVERYTHING TO ME. I
WILL NOT DIE ASHAMED. I WILL LIE
ON MY DEATHBED KNOWING THAT I
GAVE IT MY BEST SHOT,
AND EVERYTHING ELSE IS
MEANINGLESS TO ME."
LEMMY KILMISTER

Do you feel that you're living life
with integrity and if you were to die
soon, would you be satisfied with how
you lived?

OCTOBER 7

"YOU CAN'T REALLY LOVE
SOMEONE ELSE UNLESS YOU
REALLY LOVE YOURSELF FIRST."
FRED ROGERS

What do you love the most about your
unique self?

OCTOBER 8

"ALL BATTLES ARE FIRST WON OR
LOST, IN THE MIND."
JOAN OF ARC

How do you defend your mind daily
from negative people, news, gossip,
and drama?

_____

_____

_____

_____

_____

_____

OCTOBER 9

"NOTHING CAN STOP THE MAN WITH THE RIGHT MENTAL ATTITUDE FROM ACHIEVING HIS GOAL; NOTHING ON EARTH CAN HELP THE MAN WITH THE WRONG MENTAL ATTITUDE."
THOMAS JEFFERSON

What positive habits, people, music, prayers, videos, meditations, etc. do you employ daily to uplift your mindset?

OCTOBER 10

"WHEN YOU DO THINGS FROM
YOUR SOUL, YOU FEEL A RIVER
MOVING IN YOU, A JOY."
RUMI

Are you truly living your days with
joy? Explain why or why not.

_____

_____

_____

_____

_____

_____

OCTOBER 11

"I NEVER DREAMED ABOUT
SUCCESS, I WORKED FOR IT."
ESTEE LAUDER

Are you taking consistent action each
day toward your bigger goals, or do
you allow your phone or others to
continually interrupt and distract
you?

OCTOBER 12

"YOU CANNOT HANG OUT WITH
NEGATIVE PEOPLE AND EXPECT
TO LIVE A POSITIVE LIFE."
JOEL OSTEEN

Name one person in your circle who
needs to have less of your time due to
their negativity or ongoing drama.

_____

_____

_____

_____

_____

_____

OCTOBER 13

"JOY COMES TO US IN ORDINARY
MOMENTS. WE RISK MISSING OUT
WHEN WE GET TOO BUSY
CHASING DOWN THE
EXTRAORDINARY."
BRENE' BROWN

Do you schedule breaks in your day to
reset and deliberately slow down to
be aware of the bigger picture?

OCTOBER 14

"SET ASIDE JEALOUSY, ENVY, DISAPPROVAL, PAST BELIEF SYSTEMS, AND TRY COPYING EVERYTHING YOU SEE THE SUCCESSFUL DO. STUDY THEM."
DAN S. KENNEDY

Are you coachable and willing to take advice from people farther down the path than you?

OCTOBER 15

"LEAD WITH YOUR HEART AND
PUT YOUR FEAR ON THE SHELF."
TONY RUBLESKI

Do you listen to your intuition or gut,
or do you seek out other people's
opinions more than necessary?

OCTOBER 16

"THE EGO HATES LOSING –
EVEN TO GOD."
RICHARD ROHR

Do you genuinely admit to others and
yourself when you've made a
mistake?

_____

_____

_____

_____

_____

_____

_____

OCTOBER 17

"COMPARISON IS THE
THIEF OF JOY."
THEODORE ROOSEVELT

Do you realize that envy and comparison is a game you shouldn't play? Explain how you can better minimize comparisons between yourself and others.

_____

_____

_____

_____

_____

OCTOBER 18

"THE TRUTH WILL SET YOU FREE,
BUT FIRST IT WILL
PISS YOU OFF."
GLORIA STEINEM

What area of life are you in denial about that needs to change?

_____

_____

_____

_____

_____

_____

OCTOBER 19

"LITTLE THINGS APPLIED IN AN
ORGANIZED WAY, OVER TIME,
ARE THE KEY TO SUCCESS."
PAUL GUYON

What are two things that you can do
today to advance you closer to a
major goal or project you're currently
pursuing?

OCTOBER 20

"INSIST ON YOURSELF.
NEVER IMITATE."
RALPH WALDO EMERSON

What is something unique about yourself and God-given talents that you need to focus more time and energy on?

OCTOBER 21

"HOW FAR YOU GO IN LIFE DEPENDS ON
YOUR BEING TENDER WITH THE YOUNG,
COMPASSIONATE WITH THE AGED,
SYMPATHETIC WITH THE STRIVING, AND
TOLERANT OF THE WEAK AND STRONG.
BECAUSE SOMEDAY IN YOUR LIFE YOU
WILL HAVE BEEN ALL OF THESE."
GEORGE WASHINGTON CARVER

Are you understanding of others who
are at different stages and places in
life than you?

OCTOBER 22

"STOP TRYING TO CALM THE
STORM. CALM YOURSELF. THE
STORM WILL PASS."
TIMBER HAWKEYE

How do you calm yourself down in
stressful situations?

OCTOBER 23

"MANY OF US THINK THAT
COMPASSION DRAINS US, BUT I
PROMISE YOU IT IS SOMETHING
THAT TRULY ENLIVENS US."
JOAN HALIFAX

Do you take more than you give?

OCTOBER 24

"THE BITTEREST TEARS SHED
OVER GRAVES ARE FOR WORDS
LEFT UNSAID AND DEEDS LEFT
UNDONE."
HARRIET BEECHER STOWE

Who do you need to forgive today
that you've been putting off?

_____

_____

_____

_____

_____

_____

OCTOBER 25

"THE DAY YOU PLANT THE
SEED IS NOT THE DAY
YOU EAT THE FRUIT."
FABIENNE FREDRICKSON

What can you do to work on being
more patient and flexible when life
changes without warning?

OCTOBER 26

"WHEN THE WORLD FEELS LIKE AN EMOTIONAL ROLLER COASTER, STEADY YOURSELF WITH SIMPLE RITUALS. DO THE DISHES. FOLD THE LAUNDRY. WATER THE PLANTS. SIMPLICITY ATTRACTS WISDOM."
UNKNOWN

What ritual(s) do you do use to stop yourself when a negative cycle of thinking begins to appear?

OCTOBER 27

"IT'S NOT YOUR JOB TO LIKE
ME...IT'S MINE."
BYRON KATIE

What form of self-care will you
employ today to ensure you are
stronger and better equipped to
handle daily life?

_____

_____

_____

_____

_____

OCTOBER 28

"REINVENTION INVOLVES
GROWING UP. GROWING ABOVE
AND BEYOND THE HURTS AND
MEMORIES OF THE PAST."
STEVE CHANDLER

What past grievance do you need to
let go of that no longer serves you?

_____

_____

_____

_____

_____

_____

OCTOBER 29

"THE MOST PRECIOUS GIFT WE CAN
OFFER ANYONE IS OUR ATTENTION.
WHEN MINDFULNESS EMBRACES
THOSE WE LOVE, THEY WILL BLOOM
LIKE FLOWERS."
THICH NHAT HANH

Which person in your circle do you
need to spend more time with or give
attention to and why?

_____

_____

_____

_____

_____

_____

OCTOBER 30

"DON'T LET THE UGLY IN OTHERS
KILL THE BEAUTY IN YOU."
UNKNOWN

Who in your life is draining your
happiness because of their words,
attitude, and behavior toward you?

_____

_____

_____

_____

_____

_____

OCTOBER 31

"TEN YEARS FROM NOW, MAKE
SURE YOU CAN SAY YOU CHOSE
YOUR LIFE, YOU DIDN'T SETTLE
FOR IT."
MANDY HALE

What area in life are you settling for
and how can you change it?

NOVEMBER

NOVEMBER 1

"KINDNESS: LOANING SOMEONE
YOUR STRENGTH INSTEAD OF
REMINDING THEM OF THEIR
WEAKNESS."
ANDY STANLEY

Who are three people who you can
extend a kind word, call or message
to today?

_____

_____

_____

_____

_____

_____

NOVEMBER 2

"ABANDON THE IDEA THAT YOU
WILL FOREVER BE THE VICTIM OF
THE THINGS THAT HAVE
HAPPENED TO YOU. CHOOSE TO
BE A VICTOR."
SETH ADAM SMITH

Look at your current life. Are you
owning your situation and learning
from it, or using it as an excuse to
hold you back?

NOVEMBER 3

"ALTHOUGH THE WORLD IS FULL
OF SUFFERING, IT IS FULL ALSO
OF THE OVERCOMING OF IT."
HELEN KELLER

What do you do to break out of a funk
or period of sadness?

NOVEMBER 4

"EVERY CHARITABLE ACT IS A
STEPPING-STONE TOWARD
HEAVEN."
HENRY WARD BEECHER

Who in your family or at work needs
a random act of kindness from you
today?

NOVEMBER 5

"THE SIGN OF A BEAUTIFUL
PERSON IS THAT THEY ALWAYS
SEE THE BEAUTY IN OTHERS."
OMAR SULEIMAN

Do you often see the good in others,
or their faults or weaknesses?

_____

_____

_____

_____

_____

_____

NOVEMBER 6

"NURTURE YOUR MIND WITH
GREAT THOUGHTS, FOR YOU WILL
NEVER GO ANY HIGHER THAN
YOU THINK."
BENJAMIN DISRAELI

What negative habit or thought do you
need to work on removing from your
life?

_____

_____

_____

_____

_____

_____

NOVEMBER 7

"KINDNESS BEGINS WITH THE
UNDERSTANDING THAT WE ALL
STRUGGLE."
CHARLES GLASSMAN

Do you judge others too much or do
you step back and realize that no one
is perfect, including yourself?

_____

_____

_____

_____

_____

_____

NOVEMBER 8

"AT THE END OF LIFE, OUR
QUESTIONS ARE VERY SIMPLE:
DID I LIVE FULLY? DID I LOVE
WELL?"
JACK KORNFIELD

Are you truly living the life you
desire? Explain.

NOVEMBER 9

"WORRY TRADES THE JOY OF
NOW FOR THE UNLIKELY
CATASTROPHES OF LATER."
TIM FARGO

What's currently weighing in your
mind and how can lessen it?

NOVEMBER 10

"AS WE LET OUR OWN LIGHT
SHINE, WE UNCONSCIOUSLY GIVE
OTHER PEOPLE PERMISSION TO
DO THE SAME."
MARIANNE WILLIAMSON

How do you let your own light shine
each day no matter what comes your
way?

NOVEMBER 11

"EVERY TIME I JUDGE SOMEONE
ELSE, I REVEAL AN UNHEALED
PART OF MYSELF."
JOY MARINO

Are you flexible with others or stuck
in your own views of how others
should act, look, or be?

_____

_____

_____

_____

_____

_____

NOVEMBER 12

"I FOLLOW FOUR DICTATES: FACE
IT, ACCEPT IT, DEAL WITH IT,
THEN LET IT GO."
SHENG YEN

How can you apply these four dictates
to a problem you're currently facing?

_____

_____

_____

_____

_____

_____

NOVEMBER 13

"WHAT IF I FALL? OH, BUT
DARLING, WHAT IF YOU FLY?"
ERIN HANSON

When's the last time you set a big
goal in your life and took at least 60
days to attack it and pursue it?
Explain how you could make time for
this approach for your next goal.

NOVEMBER 14

"DON'T TELL SOMEONE TO GET
OVER IT. HELP THEM GET
THROUGH IT."
SUE FITZMAURICE

Do you lead by jumping in the trenches to help or do you spout off words and clichés not backed up by action?

NOVEMBER 15

"THE REAL SECRET IS WHEN YOU
TURN INWARD FOR WISDOM AND
PEACE."
TONY RUBLESKI

Do you incorporate prayer, quiet
time, or meditation into your daily
life?

NOVEMBER 16

"LIFE BECOMES EASIER WHEN
YOU LEARN TO ACCEPT AN
APOLOGY YOU NEVER GOT."
ROBERT BRAULT

Which person in your present or past
is long overdue to be forgiven or
made amends with?

_____

_____

_____

_____

_____

_____

NOVEMBER 17

"GOD GAVE YOU THE GIFT OF
86,400 SECONDS TODAY. HAVE
YOU USED ONE TO SAY 'THANK
YOU'?"
WILLIAM WARD

Who are three people you need to thank before your head hits the pillow tonight?

_____

_____

_____

_____

_____

_____

NOVEMBER 18

"IT IS ONLY WITH GRATITUDE
THAT LIFE BECOMES RICH."
DIETRICH BONHOEFFER

What are five things, situations, or
people that you are grateful for?

_____

_____

_____

_____

_____

_____

NOVEMBER 19

"IF WE ARE EVER TO ENJOY LIFE
NOW IS THE TIME, NOT
TOMORROW OR NEXT YEAR."
THOMAS DREIER

If you knew you'd be dead by
tomorrow, how would you approach
the next 24 hours?

NOVEMBER 20

"WHEN YOU ARISE IN THE
MORNING THINK OF WHAT A
PRIVILEGE IT IS TO BE ALIVE, TO
THINK, TO ENJOY, TO LOVE."
MARCUS AURELIUS

Are you grateful for this exact
moment or are you taking life for
granted? How can you be grateful for
today?

NOVEMBER 21

"WHEN YOU BLAME OTHERS, YOU
GIVE UP YOUR POWER TO
CHANGE."
DR. ROBERT ANTHONY

What grudge is holding you back
toward living a happier life?

NOVEMBER 22

"WHEN IT COMES TO LIFE THE
CRITICAL THING IS WHETHER YOU
TAKE THINGS FOR GRANTED OR
TAKE THEM WITH GRATITUDE."
G.K. CHESTERTON

Who or what are you taking for
granted and how can you change that?

NOVEMBER 23

"IF YOU'RE NOT HAVING A
GOOD TIME, FIND SOMETHING
ELSE THAT GIVES YOU
SOME JOY IN LIFE."
PENNY MARSHALL

Is your life filled with more joy than
disappointment?

NOVEMBER 24

"REFLECT UPON YOUR PRESENT
BLESSINGS OF WHICH EVERY MAN
HAS PLENTY; NOT ON YOUR PAST
MISFORTUNES OF WHICH ALL
MEN HAVE SOME."
CHARLES DICKENS

List ten things in your life that you
are grateful for.

NOVEMBER 25

"WE MUST FIND THE TIME TO STOP AND THANK THE PEOPLE WHO MAKE A DIFFERENCE IN OUR LIVES."
JOHN F. KENNEDY

Think about those who've made the biggest impact in your life or career. Who are they and how can you thank them today?

NOVEMBER 26

"THE HIGHEST TRIBUTE TO THE
DEAD IS NOT GRIEF BUT
GRATITUDE."
THORNTON WILDER

If you died today, what would people
say about you? Would they be
grateful and respect you for being in
their life and how you treated them?

NOVEMBER 27

"OPTIMISTS FIND JOY IN SMALL
THINGS. THEY ARE MORE
CONCERNED WITH HAVING MANY
SMALL JOYS RATHER THAN
HAVING ONE HUGE JOY."
ROBERT M. SHERFIELD

What small joys do you see and enjoy
each day?

NOVEMBER 28

"ACKNOWLEDGING THE GOOD
THAT YOU ALREADY HAVE IN
YOUR LIFE IS THE FOUNDATION
FOR ALL ABUNDANCE."
ECKHART TOLLE

Are you happy now or waiting on
something in the future to make you
happy or feel better?

_____

_____

_____

_____

_____

NOVEMBER 29

"IT ISN'T WHAT YOU HAVE, OR WHO
YOU ARE, OR WHERE YOU ARE, OR
WHAT YOU ARE DOING THAT MAKES
YOU HAPPY OR UNHAPPY. IT IS
WHAT YOU THINK ABOUT."
DALE CARNEGIE

Are you managing your thoughts
wisely and with happiness or are you
too often influenced by negative
people, habits, and opinions?

NOVEMBER 30

"YOU WILL HAVE BAD TIMES, BUT
THEY WILL ALWAYS WAKE YOU
UP TO THE STUFF YOU WEREN'T
PAYING ATTENTION TO."
ROBIN WILLIAMS

What adversity have you recently
experienced that was a needed wake-
up call?

_____

_____

_____

_____

_____

_____

DECEMBER

DECEMBER 1

"NEVER BLAME ANYONE IN YOUR
LIFE. GOOD PEOPLE GIVE YOU
HAPPINESS. BAD PEOPLE GIVE YOU
EXPERIENCE. WORST PEOPLE GIVE
YOU A LESSON. AND BEST PEOPLE
GIVE YOU MEMORIES."
ZIG ZIGLAR

Who or what in your life brings you happiness? Who has taught you a valuable lesson? What great memories do you have and what can draw from all of it?

_____

_____

_____

_____

_____

DECEMBER 2

"PLENTY OF PEOPLE MISS THEIR SHARE OF HAPPINESS, NOT BECAUSE THEY NEVER FOUND IT, BUT BECAUSE THEY DIDN'T STOP TO ENJOY IT."
WILLIAM FEATHER

When's the last time you sat down, reflected, took a deep breath, and truly gave thanks to God for the life you have been given? How can you make it a daily habit?

_____

_____

_____

_____

_____

DECEMBER 3

"IT'S THE POSSIBILITY OF
HAVING A DREAM COME TRUE
THAT MAKES LIFE INTERESTING."
PAULO COELHO

Do you still dream about what you
want or how life could be? What is
your current dream?

_____

_____

_____

_____

_____

_____

DECEMBER 4

"MOST OF US HAVE TWO LIVES.
THE LIFE WE LIVE, AND THE
UNLIVED LIFE WITHIN US.
BETWEEN THE TWO STANDS
RESISTANCE."
STEVEN PRESSFIELD

What negative thought or habit is stopping you right now from having a better life?

DECEMBER 5

"THIS IS A BRIEF LIFE, BUT IN ITS
BREVITY IT OFFERS US SOME
SPLENDID MOMENTS, SOME
MEANINGFUL ADVENTURES."
RUDYARD KIPLING

What are five incredible joys or
memories in your life journey that
make you smile when you think about
them?

DECEMBER 6

"GREAT ACHIEVEMENT IS
USUALLY BORN OF GREAT
SACRIFICE AND IS NEVER THE
RESULT OF SELFISHNESS."
NAPOLEON HILL

What sacrifices are you willing to
make to achieve your goals?

DECEMBER 7

"IN EVERY WALK WITH NATURE
ONE RECEIVES FAR MORE
THAN HE SEEKS."
JOHN MUIR

When's the last time you unplugged,
got off the grid, and took a long walk
to clear your body, mind, and spirit?

DECEMBER 8

"WHEN I STAND BEFORE GOD AT
THE END OF MY LIFE, I WOULD
HOPE THAT I WOULD NOT HAVE A
SINGLE BIT OF TALENT LEFT, AND
COULD SAY, 'I USED EVERYTHING
YOU GAVE ME'. "
ERMA BOMBECK

Are you using your best talents to
their full potential?

DECEMBER 9

"THE HUMAN SPIRIT, LIKE A
CAMPFIRE, MUST BE LIT
AGAIN EACH DAY."
STEVE CHANDLER

Do you start the day with a ritual or
action to inspire yourself, or do you
awake, check your phone, and shift
into reaction mode?

DECEMBER 10

"SHARE YOUR SMILE WITH THE WORLD. IT'S A SYMBOL OF FRIENDSHIP AND PEACE."
CHRISTIE BRINKLEY

Do you smile at most people when you see them or pass by them? Do you seek to connect and make others feel welcome and at ease?

DECEMBER 11

"ASSOCIATE YOURSELF WITH
PEOPLE OF GOOD QUALITY, FOR
IT IS BETTER TO BE ALONE THAN
IN BAD COMPANY."
BOOKER T. WASHINGTON

Who do you look up to as a positive
force in your life that you should
spend more time with?

_____

_____

_____

_____

_____

_____

DECEMBER 12

"TO ONE WHO HAS FAITH, NO EXPLANATION IS NECESSARY. TO ONE WITHOUT FAITH, NO EXPLANATION IS POSSIBLE."
THOMAS AQUINAS

Has life turned you into a doubting Thomas or do you still believe in miracles?

DECEMBER 13

"IT TAKES MORE THAN JUST A
GOOD LOOKING BODY. YOU'VE
GOT TO HAVE THE HEART AND
SOUL TO GO WITH IT."
EPICTETUS

Are you well-rounded with your
personal development or too focused
in one area?

_____

_____

_____

_____

_____

_____

DECEMBER 14

"YOU HAVE TO PUT IN MANY, MANY, MANY TINY EFFORTS THAT NOBODY SEES OR APPRECIATES BEFORE YOU ACHIEVE ANYTHING WORTHWHILE."
BRIAN TRACY

What are some of the tiny efforts required for you to successfully complete your next goal?

_____

_____

_____

_____

_____

DECEMBER 15

"JUST WHEN YOU THINK YOU'VE REACHED ROCK BOTTOM, GOD HAS THE POWER TO LIFT YOU RIGHT BACK UP."
TONY RUBLESKI

Do you push ahead with faith when you hit resistance, or do you let fear and doubt slow you down?

DECEMBER 16

"THE GREAT AIM OF EDUCATION
IS NOT KNOWLEDGE
BUT ACTION."
HERBERT SPENCER

Do you spend too much time
researching and preparing, or do you
set deadlines and take action?

_____

_____

_____

_____

_____

DECEMBER 17

"HAPPINESS IS NOT SOMETHING
YOU POSTPONE FOR THE FUTURE;
IT IS SOMETHING YOU DESIGN
FOR THE PRESENT."
JIM ROHN

How can you live for today and not
take the future for granted?

_____

_____

_____

_____

_____

_____

DECEMBER 18

"MAKE GENEROSITY A PART OF
YOUR GROWTH STRATEGY."
DANIELLE LAPORTE

What can you do today to show
someone special in your life that you
are grateful for them?

_____

_____

_____

_____

_____

_____

DECEMBER 19

"START WITH GOD. THE FIRST
STEP IN LEARNING IS BOWING
DOWN TO GOD; ONLY FOOLS
THUMB THEIR NOSES AT SUCH
WISDOM AND LEARNING."
KING SOLOMON

Is God an afterthought or common
presence within your daily life?

_____

_____

_____

_____

_____

_____

_____

DECEMBER 20

"OPTIMISM IS THE MOST
IMPORTANT HUMAN TRAIT,
BECAUSE IT ALLOWS US TO
EVOLVE OUR IDEAS, TO IMPROVE
OUR SITUATION, AND TO HOPE FOR
A BETTER TOMORROW."
SETH GODIN

Do you look at life with more of the glass-half-full or the glass-half-empty mindset?

DECEMBER 21

"YOUR TIME, ENERGY, AND
MONEY ALWAYS GO TO WHAT'S
IMPORTANT TO YOU."
LARRY WINGET

Is your money focused on temporary
pleasures or significant experiences
that create powerful meaning?

DECEMBER 22

"TRUE FREEDOM IS IMPOSSIBLE
WITHOUT A MIND MADE FREE BY
DISCIPLINE."
MORTIMER J. ADLER

What new daily habit could you look
to add into your life that would help
you be more focused and disciplined?

_____

_____

_____

_____

_____

_____

DECEMBER 23

"SUCCESS IS NOT MEASURED BY WHAT
YOU ACCOMPLISH, BUT BY THE
OPPOSITION YOU HAVE ENCOUNTERED,
AND THE COURAGE WITH WHICH YOU
HAVE MAINTAINED THE STRUGGLE
AGAINST OVERWHELMING ODDS."
ORISON SWETT MARDEN

What major challenge or problem in
your life have you solved or overcome
in the past 6 months? What was the
main takeaway?

DECEMBER 24

"IT'S NOT THE STRENGTH OF THE
BODY THAT COUNTS, BUT THE
STRENGTH OF THE SPIRIT."
J.R.R. TOLKIEN

How strong is your spiritual life?

_____

_____

_____

_____

_____

_____

_____

DECEMBER 25

"THE WAY TO GET STARTED IS TO
QUIT TALKING
AND BEGIN DOING."
WALT DISNEY

What goal or dream have you put been
putting off and why?

DECEMBER 26

"GOD'S DELAYS ARE NOT
GOD'S DENIALS."
ROBERT H. SCHULLER

What can you do to release the grip of expectations when you run into delay or setbacks?

_____

_____

_____

_____

_____

_____

DECEMBER 27

"A GOAL SHOULD SCARE YOU A
LITTLE AND EXCITE YOU A LOT."
DR. JOE VITALE

What's your next goal? How much
does it scare you and excite you?

_____

_____

_____

_____

_____

_____

DECEMBER 28

"WE ARE HERE TO CHANGE. WE
ARE HERE TO GROW, DEVELOP
AND UNFOLD. WE ARE
PROGRESSIVE BEINGS THAT HAVE
INFINITE CAPACITY."
MICHAEL BECKWITH

How do you view change and wha
can you do to handle it better?

DECEMBER 29

"WHETHER YOU BE MAN OR
WOMAN YOU WILL NEVER DO
ANYTHING IN THIS WORLD
WITHOUT COURAGE. IT IS THE
GREATEST QUALITY OF THE MIND
NEXT TO HONOR."
JAMES ALLEN

When's the last time you tried
something new that you were initially
scared or worried about attempting?

_____

_____

_____

_____

_____

_____

DECEMBER 30

"NEVER BLAME YOURSELF FOR
SOMEONE'S SUFFERING. MANY
HAVE BECOME VETERANS IN
SUFFERING."
SADHGURU

Who in your life is constantly a woe-
is-me person? How can you cut back
your time with them?

_____

_____

_____

_____

_____

_____

DECEMBER 31

"A YEAR AGO, YOU DID NOT
KNOW TODAY. YOU DID NOT
KNOW HOW YOU'D MAKE IT HERE.
BUT YOU MADE IT HERE. BY
GRACE, YOU MADE IT HERE."
MORGAN HARPER NICHOLS

What are you most grateful for in the
past year and what excites you for the
year ahead?

_____

_____

_____

_____

_____

_____

About the Author

Tony Rubleski, Mind Capture Group

Tony is currently the president of Mind Capture Group. His message is designed to help people 'Capture' more minds and profits. He is an in-demand speaker who's given hundreds of presentations, strategic business coach, and creator of the Mind Capture Bootcamp now in its 10th year. He has over 25+ years of experience in the personal development industry.

His Mind Capture book series has spawned multiple bestsellers in a variety of business and coaching categories with Amazon.com.